What people are

# The Art of Li....

What a wonderful book with so much detail packed in about this fascinating form of divination. The author takes you through the whole process of creating your own set of lithomancy stones, how to pick them, work with them and keep them magical. There are lots of suggestions for different sets along with ideas and guidelines to help you get the best from reading with them. Highly recommended.

**Rachel Patterson**, Author of the *Kitchen Witch* series, *Witchcraft into the Wilds* and several books in the *Pagan Portals* series

Jessica's book is a completely accessible introduction to lithomancy, making the subject both intriguing yet simple to learn. Notes on the history of lithomancy enrich the text, and the way she encourages and empowers readers to trust their own intuition is inspiring. Methods for connecting with the stones, cleansing them, and making this practice your own run throughout the book, creating an ideal volume for anyone interested in divination, regardless of their own personal path. I look forward to gathering my own set of stones, and exploring this mysterious yet effective divination technique.

**Mabh Savage**, Author of *A Modern Celt* and *Practically Pagan: An Alternative Guide to Planet Friendly Living*

This is the perfect book for anyone who is looking to find a way into divining in general and Lithomancy in particular. Aimed at beginners it is a thorough guide to the art of divining with stones of all kinds. Howard carefully avoids being prescriptive allowing the reader to explore and find their own way of developing a practice. It would also be eminently suitable for anyone who already divines but who is interested in expanding their range and learning how to work closely with stones. A great addition to the resources available for those learning to divine.

**Yvonne Ryves**, Author of *Shaman Pathways – Web of Life*, Retired Shamanic Healer, Reiki Master and Past Life Therapist

*The Art of Lithomancy* by Jessica Howard is a detailed guidebook on the art of stone divination. An enjoyable book that makes this form of divination accessible to all.

**Jennifer Teixeira**, Author of *Temple of the Bones: Rituals to the Goddess Hekate*

Pagan Portals

# The Art of Lithomancy

Pagan Portals

# The Art of Lithomancy

Jessica Howard

MOON
BOOKS

Winchester, UK
Washington, USA

JOHN HUNT PUBLISHING

First published by Moon Books, 2022
Moon Books is an imprint of John Hunt Publishing Ltd., No. 3 East Street, Alresford
Hampshire SO24 9EE, UK
office@jhpbooks.net
www.johnhuntpublishing.com
www.moon-books.net

For distributor details and how to order please visit the 'Ordering' section on our website.

ISBN: 978 1 78904 914 5
978 1 78904 915 2 (ebook)
Library of Congress Control Number: 2021937386

A CIP catalogue record for this book is available from the British Library.

Design: Matthew Greenfield

UK: Printed and bound by CPI Group (UK) Ltd, Croydon, CR0 4YY
Printed in North America by CPI GPS partners

We operate a distinctive and ethical publishing philosophy in
all areas of our business, from our global network of authors to
production and worldwide distribution.

# Contents

James – thank you so much for all of your support over the years. And for never complaining despite the random piles of stones, crystals, and shells lying around the house! I couldn't have done this without you.

Emmie and Sinead – thank you for your continued enthusiasm and cheering me on.

# Preface

My name is Jess and I've been a practicing witch for roughly 20 years now. I started off with Wicca which has led me down many different paths since then. These days my path is definitely best described as eclectic! Heavily influenced by Water Witchcraft, there are also elements of Kitchen Witchcraft, Celtic Witchcraft, and Green Witchcraft thrown in. A connection with the local land and the spirits that reside there is extremely important to me and although I live in the city, I am lucky enough to live next to lots of green spaces.

I have been a part of several in-person groups but recently have tended to operate mostly online. One of those online activities is as an elder and mentor as a part of an online coven and it is thanks to this group that this book exists. As an elder, one of the courses I taught was an introduction to lithomancy. It was at this time that I realized that there was very little information out there on lithomancy, and seeing as I had a lot of the information already put together, a book seemed like a logical next step. So, I want to say a huge thanks to the founder of the Pagan Mentorship Programme, Jules, and all those original students for helping shape the course of this book.

I was first introduced to lithomancy at a workshop run by The Kitchen Witchcraft School of Natural Witchery a few years ago, and from that very first moment it just clicked with me. I read any information I could find the subject, built my own sets and experimented with different methods of interpretation. Some worked, some did not. I endeavoured to take a traditional practice, which to date didn't have much information available on it, and make it accessible for anyone who wanted to give it a go.

If there is one thing I have learned about lithomancy, it is that there really is no right or wrong way of doing it. Everything I have written in this book should be used as a framework upon which to build your own way of performing lithomancy. There are some commonly accepted standards of interpretation such as the meanings behind certain patterns and the associations of the planetary influences if you choose to use that method. However, this doesn't mean that you need to restrict yourself to these if you find that they don't work for you. You may find different patterns or different ways of interpreting different layouts which I haven't talked about, because they are unique to you. What I hope you get most out of this book is the knowledge and the confidence to start using your intuition to forge your own path.

As well as acting as an elder and mentor in an online coven, I also run my own website www.thecottagemystic.com, and you can find me on Instagram at @thecottagemysticwitch.

# Chapter 1

# What Is Lithomancy?

The art of lithomancy is one which many people are aware of, although they may not know the name of it. The most common definition of lithomancy is the art of divination by reading stones. It involves the caster, or the diviner, 'throwing' stones and then divining the future based on both where the stones fall in relation to each other, and the patterns in which they fall. It is a simple yet extremely insightful method that relies on nothing but some easily accessible tools and your intuition. This is the beauty of lithomancy; you don't need to spend a ridiculous amount of money on buying exactly the right kit (although there is nothing wrong with buying a pre-made kit), or to take a specific course to qualify as a 'master' at the expense of your bank account. It is easily accessible and easy to get to grips with, but don't let this simplicity fool you; it is extremely effective.

I have tried many different divination methods, such as runes, tarot, pendulum, oracle cards, scrying, bird divination and more. But I can honestly say that lithomancy has been one which, from the first reading I ever did, just clicked with me. It is perfect for those who may be new or those who are looking to find a divination method they can learn and grow with.

Lithomancy commonly uses stones and crystals. However, you can use anything that has symbolic meaning to you (providing it is a suitable size and weight); coins, shells, charms, bones, etc. One of the many great things about lithomancy is that you can really tailor it to your own personal symbolism, get creative, and have fun with it.

It is said that the earliest verified account of lithomancy being used stretches right back to the Romans, in the city of Constantinople around the 800's. The Patriarch of Constantinople,

Photus, describes how a physician named Eusebius used a stone known as a baetulum (often formed from a piece of meteorite) to perform a ritual to divine the future. In this tale, Eusebius, having suddenly developed an urge to climb to the top of a mountain to the temple of Minerva, lay resting after his climb. From there he saw a sphere of fire falling from the sky down to the earth and a lion standing next to where it had landed. The lion disappeared as the fire was extinguished and there lay the baetulum. Roughly the size of the palm of the hand, baetulum's are often white although sometimes purple in color. The one which Eusebius found would answer questions by emitting a shrill sound which he would then interpret.

A similar story recounts how Helenus used lithomancy to predict the destruction of Troy. It is recorded that the God Apollo gave Helenus a stone (or sometimes a magnet). After performing several rites which included washing the stone or magnet in the water from a spring, it finally spoke to him and told him of the fall of Troy.

The two stories, which are both attributed to being the earliest examples of lithomancy, are quite different to the lithomancy technique which is often meant of when we speak of it today. Aside from these two instances, there is a real lack of any clear historical records around the art of lithomancy. There are other books and websites that say the Celts used lithomancy or that it became well established in the medieval period. However, finding actual historical evidence of these claims is very difficult, and its history, practices, and the origins of lithomancy as we know it today remain a mystery.

It is one of the reasons I felt compelled to write this book. Simply searching through Amazon will show very few modern resources on lithomancy. It is a divination practice suitable for all levels, and deserves to be given more attention than it currently seems to receive. This book is a combination of research and my own personal experience with lithomancy, and includes more traditional methods and modern ones. From choosing your stones, to assigning meanings, interpreting readings, and performing readings for others, this book should contain everything you need to get started.

So, what exactly can lithomancy tell us? Like many forms of divination, lithomancy can help us understand our past and our present. It can help us divine the future, uncover ancient knowledge and wisdom, connect with our higher selves, and unlock the secrets of our subconscious. Whilst the majority of this book is dedicated to using lithomancy as a divination technique, I have also written a section on how you can use lithomancy and the energy of the chakras to help heal and understand where best to focus your energies. Whilst this is a bit of a detour from the traditional way in which lithomancy is used, I have found it extremely effective and couldn't not share it with you all!

We cast our stones and interpret readings both by looking at the where the stones fall and the patterns they fall in, and by using our intuition to listen to the message of the stones. Anybody can learn lithomancy. All you need is a little bit of patience and plenty of practice. There are many different ways to perform lithomancy, from simple 'yes' and 'no' answers, to working with astrological influences, or using charts to help with your divination. We will be looking at all of these to help you find the method that best suits you.

## What Is Intuition?

Before we go any further let's take a look at 'intuition'. You will notice that I use the word intuition a lot in this book as it is primarily our intuition we use to interpret our readings. But what exactly is the intuition, and how do you use it?

There is no one universally accepted definition of what intuition is. I know that quoting from the Dictionary is generally an overdone trope, but in this case, it really does provide a great definition of what we mean when we talk about intuition:

Simply type 'definition of intuition' into google.co.uk, and it will provide the following:

*The ability to understand something instinctively, without the need for conscious reasoning. (https://www.google.co.uk, 2021)*

It is an innate feeling. If you try to rationalize it, you have already lost it. This is important to bear in mind when we interpret our readings. When you are reading your stones, often a meaning or message will pop into your mind first. Even if you have to refer to your notes and remind yourself of the meanings of each stone, always go with the particular meaning which resonates with you most strongly. This is your intuition talking to you. Don't ignore it. If you start second-guessing yourself you can easily become confused and find yourself struggling to work out what the stones are trying to tell you.

There are many different ways to strengthen your intuition and lots of books, online articles, and videos on the subject. Meditation is a great skill to learn but the best way to improve it is to use it. Listen to your gut instinct, that voice that first pops into your head, and see where it leads you.

Now let's get started!

# Chapter 2

# Getting Started

## Your Set

In this section we will be looking at everything you need to build to actually performing a reading. There are three main different methods of lithomancy:

**Yes/No Set:** The yes/no set is very straight forward. For this, you will need at least two stones, one to represent 'yes' and one to represent 'no'. You may wish to add an additional stone to represent a 'maybe' answer and potentially a personal stone. I'll talk about what your personal stone is and what it does a little further on in the book.

**Astrological Correspondences Set:** Possibly the most well-known form, this set-up is made up of thirteen or sixteen stones in total. Traditionally seven stones represent different planetary influences – the Sun, the Moon, Mars, Venus, Mercury, Jupiter and Saturn. The remaining six represent a place, love, magic, life, luck and commitment. However, some modern sets include an additional three planetary stones to bring the total number of stones to sixteen – Uranus, Neptune, and Pluto. It is up to you whether you want to work with seven or ten planetary stones.

**'Freestyle' Sets:** I'm calling these freestyle sets because that is exactly what they are – there are no rules, no limitations, only the ones you impose on yourself. You can buy them online or make your own. They can contain anything you want, not just stones, and you can have as many or as few items as you want. You can have any meanings or associations assigned to them. This is personally my favorite type of lithomancy and the first set I ever used was one I had created myself in a lithomancy workshop. I will take you through how to choose your own stones and items, as well as how to cleanse and empower them, and assign your own meanings to them. Essentially, the way you use these three different sets is the same so the rest of this book is relevant no matter which type you choose to use.

When thinking about which set to start off with there are a few things you may wish to consider. First, how much time do you have to invest in this? If you are keen to get going and have access to stones, crystals, etc., then a yes/no set, or the astrological correspondences set might be best. Having the messages and meanings already laid out for you will save a lot of time. Or maybe the idea of getting to create your own set from scratch is so appealing that you would much rather take the additional time to get your own set just right. I personally find this the most rewarding way to work. Experimenting with different stones and different combinations of meanings is a lot of fun, and finding a set which you really gel with is such a satisfying feeling. One of the bonuses of creating your own set is you can have as many or as few stones as you want, and can add more in the future as your confidence grows.

## Choosing the Right Stones

No matter which type of lithomancy set you choose to work with you will need to find a number of items to cast in your reading. Remember, whilst stones and crystals are traditionally used for lithomancy, you can choose other objects you would like. To make it easier I will just refer to 'stones' in this book, but what you use is up to you. Try to make sure that they are all roughly the same size, the same weight, and are hardy enough that they won't damage when cast.

If you wish to use crystals, try and choose those that share the same qualities as the meaning you want to assign each one. For example, if you want a crystal to represent intuition in your reading then you could use one such as amethyst. If you would like a crystal to represent masculine energy then you could use a crystal such as goldstone or sunstone. If, instead of crystals, you want to use charms and other objects, again try to find objects that physically symbolize their associations, as this will make them easier to work with. A heart shaped charm could represent love, and a thimble, usually used for sewing, could represent the home or creative arts.

This does present us with a bit of a 'chicken and egg' scenario. You could decide on which stones you want to use first and then assign meanings based on the associations of that stone. Or you could decide on the meanings you want represented in your set and then choose the stones which are associated with those meanings. Whichever way you want to do it is up to you. If you wish to choose the stones and then choose the meanings based on the stones then carry on reading. However, if you want to decide on the meanings first and then use those to determine which stones you use in your kit, it may be best to jump ahead to the *Assigning Meanings* section, and then returning to the *Choosing The Right Stones* section. Designing your own set is a personal experience so don't rush the process; take your time and enjoy it!

If you wish to use stones, pebbles, shells, or other 'natural' objects you can pick these from your garden, park, beach etc. Go for a walk with your intent in mind and let yourself be drawn to certain objects as you go. You could even make a mini ritual out of it to help strengthen your intent; for example, you may wish to light a silver or purple candle, and as you focus on your intent say a little incantation such as *"please help me to find the stones I need to perform this divination"* before you leave the house. You can make this a prayer to a specific deity if you wish, or you can simply state your intention to the universe.

If you are using regular stones or pebbles then you can decorate them to symbolize their associations and make it easier to tell them apart in readings. Also make a note of any little oddities of characteristics of the stones you are using, such as cracks, points, bumps, rough patches, etc. These can be used in your interpretation and I'll talk a little more on that when we get to the chapter about performing your reading.

Many sets tend to contain thirteen stones but you can have as few or as many as you want. Using more stones doesn't necessarily mean more accurate readings – I've seen lithomancy sets that contain sixty items to cast with which definitely feels a bit extreme for a beginner (and to be honest, even a bit intimidating for someone like me who has been practicing for several years). Don't be afraid to add or remove stones or objects as you practice and discover what works best for you.

You can have different sets for different intentions or different types of reading. For example, I use the set that I first created as my 'general' reading set and readings I perform for other people. However, I also have another set made from sea glass, shells, and small pebbles I found on the beach which I use specifically for readings centred around my emotional state and related outcomes. There is no limit to how many sets you create, how many stones you use, or the meanings you assign them.

Take some time to think about the objects you want to use in your lithomancy set. Are you planning on using regular stones and pebbles and if so, are you going to decorate them? Or maybe you would prefer to use crystals? Would you like to add any other additions, such as shells or coins to the set? If at this stage you want to choose your stones and then assign meanings to them, then start collecting your kit together. If you would prefer to figure out the meanings first and then choose suitable stones/crystals/charms based on those meanings, then make sure you read the *assigning meanings* section before completing this step.

Another question worth asking yourself at this stage is around the main types of readings you would like to do with your set. Are you going to start out with general life readings, or maybe you are interested in lithomancy to help you with matters related to your love life or financial welfare? This can also help you determine that types of stones/crystals/charms/etc., to include in your kit and their meanings. You might decide to create a set which is specific to readings around relationships and love, or a set which is specific to readings around your spiritual growth, or any other aspect of your life that is important to you. However, I recommend every practitioner have a general 'life reading' set, so this is a good starting point if you are practicing lithomancy for the first time.

## Choosing Your Personal Stone

The decision to use a personal stone or not is – well – personal! A personal stone represents 'you' in a reading. The reading is conducted by looking at how the stones fall in relation to your personal stone. If you choose to use a personal stone then try and pick a stone, crystal or object that has some sort of symbolism to you, or you have a connection with. I use a piece of lodestone as my personal stone; its magnetic properties make me think of 'drawing' the correct stones and energies to myself in my reading. You may wish to use a crystal that you are particularly drawn to, or a stone which you have decorated specifically with colours and symbols which have meaning to you.

Whatever you decide to use for your personal stone, I recommend carrying it around with you so you can attune to its energy and it can attune to yours. Meditate with it, sleep with it under your pillow, and even bathe with it for a few days if you can. The stronger connection you build with your personal stone, the better it will serve you.

If you decide to create multiple lithomancy sets then you can use the same personal stone across all sets, or have a different stone for each set. I personally have a different stone for each set, but that is just because that is what feels right to me. If you don't want to use a personal stone, then instead, you will focus on the stones which fall closest to you when you do your reading. We will talk more about this later on when we discuss performing readings.

If you are going to be creating a yes/no set, then the decision as to whether to use a personal stone is up to you. If you are going to be trying out the astrological correspondences set, it traditionally doesn't use a personal stone – however, there is no reason you can't add one in if you would like.

Don't rush when thinking about your personal stone. What exactly is it going to be, a stone, a crystal, a shell, etc? If so, are there any particular 'types' that call to you? Are you going to decorate it and if so, what has personal meaning to you that you could incorporate into the design? Do you want your personal stone to 'stand out' from the rest of the stones – for example, if you are creating a kit made entirely of shells then perhaps you would like your personal stone to instead be a crystal.

## Cleansing Your Stones

Now you have chosen the stones, crystals or other symbolic items you will use in your set, you need to cleanse them before charging them to imbue them with the power of your association and intent. Cleansing is very important, whether you are making your own set or have brought one online. It will clear the stones of any negative energy and essentially create a blank slate for you to start from. From there, you can assign your meanings and associations to the stones and start to connect with their energy.

There are several different methods you can choose from when cleansing your stones. Try to pick a method which is suitable for the material you are using. Some crystals don't react well to water, so you might be best using a different method than holding them under running water. Below are some quick and easy ways of cleansing:

- Pass them through the smoke of incense. You could choose incense which is renowned for its cleansing properties such as frankincense, sandalwood, sage or lavender.

- Hold them under running water for a couple of minutes whilst visualising any negativity being washed away. In an ideal world unfiltered spring water would be ideal, but I have never had any problem just holding my stones under a tap in the bathroom to cleanse them. You could also use moon water, rain water, or sea water as all are great for cleansing.

- Bury them in earth for twenty-four hours. Note: this approach can be messy, and if your stones have any cracks in them, then there is a chance earth could get stuck in them.

- Cleanse them in the light of a full moon. As the moon represents intuition, divination, and psychic abilities then this would be a very apt approach. Simply leave your stones on a windowsill or some other place where they will be bathed in the light of the full moon until morning.

Although this isn't entirely necessary, if you would like to add a bit more formality to the process, I have a more structured ritual using the five elements you can perform to cleanse your stones. Personally, I find that this formality helps to establish intent and creates a stronger bond between you and your stones. This ritual is fairly basic and pretty standard for cleansing. Chances are that you will have come across it before in some form or another, but this is my interpretation of it.

You will need:
    A candle
    A bowl or cup of water
    Salt
    Incense
    A pentacle; you can even just draw one onto a piece of paper if you like.

I prefer to do each stone individually although you may wish to do them in groups of three, especially if you have a large number of stones or are short on time. The first step is to ground yourself. Imagine your feet like roots, flowing deep into the earth beneath you. They anchor you to the earth and connect you, keeping you stable and allowing you to draw energy up from the earth as well as send it back down.

Take a deep breath, clear your mind. Pick up your first stone (or stones), hold it aloft and say:

*I come here now to cleanse this stone, in the name of the Great Goddess, the keeper of mysteries and the bringer of truth. May it be rid of all negativity.*

I generally use the Goddess, but you may wish to use a specific deity, the God, or even just Spirit or Universal Energy. Substitute 'Goddess' for whichever feels more comfortable for you. Take a pinch of salt and sprinkle it over the stone and say:

*With the element of earth, I cleanse this stone of all negativity in this world and in the astral.*

Now pass it through your incense smoke and say:

*With the element of air, I cleanse this stone of all negativity in this world and in the astral.*

Pass it over the flame of the candle and say:

*With the element of fire, I cleanse this stone of all negativity in this world and in the astral.*

Sprinkle some of the water over it and say:

*With the element of water, I cleanse this stone of all negativity, in this world and in the astral.*

With every element, visualize it cleansing any negative energies from the stone you are holding. I tend to imagine that salt dissolves the negativity, air blows it away, fire burns it, and water washes it away. Place the stone in the middle of the pentacle. Repeat this until all the stones have been passed through all four elements and then sit in the middle of the pentacle.

Now visualize a pillar of white light coming down from the skies, shining upon your stones. This is the light of the Goddess (or whoever you are calling upon), pure and cleansing, removing all negativity and blessing your stones with their power. If it helps, hold your hands over the stones and visualize the energy being channelled through your body, down through your arms and out through your hands into the stones. Or you can place your fingers in a triangle shape over the stones and visualize the energy being focused through this point and into the stones. When you feel ready, say:

*In the name of the Great Goddess, she who reveals the hidden truths and casts light upon all that is unknown, I cleanse and bless these stones of all negativity, that they may be used to divine the future and help me see the unseen. So mote it be!*

## Assigning Meanings

The next step is to assign meanings to your individual stones, and for that you need to know exactly what their associations are going to be. If you are using the astrological associations for your stones then these have set meanings, which you can find a bit further on in the book. First though, we will take a look at coming up with your own messages and meanings.

How in depth you go with this is completely up to you. I've seen descriptions of meanings which are pages and pages long, and I've seen descriptions which are literally just one key word. I would recommend, especially if you are a beginner, that you find a happy-medium between these two extremes. Just having one key word assigned to each stone is very restrictive when it comes to performing a reading, whilst having too many meanings assigned to one stone can become confusing and make it difficult to interpret.

Keywords or key sentences are a great way to start and provide a foundation from which you can expand on the meanings and messages behind each stone. Think about the sorts of questions you want to ask your set; will you mostly be asking questions about life in general? Will you mostly be asking questions about your relationships with others? If so, what kind of answers or guidance could you be looking for the stones to give you?

For example, the lithomancy set that I created specifically to bring me insight into issues of the emotional self has stones with key words such as 'emotional balance', 'relationships', 'making peace and moving on' and 'making difficult decisions'.

You can assign more than one keyword to a stone but make sure that they are related. As above, 'making peace' and 'moving on' work well because they often go hand-in-hand. However, assigning one stone both the meanings of 'wealth' and 'communication' could be so far removed from one another that it will make it difficult to know which meaning is relevant in the readings you are doing.

I've listed some common keywords below as a starting point to give you an idea as to what you could potentially include in your own set. Remember that this is just a guide to help you on your way – you can add anything you want as long as it has relevance to you. At the back of this book I have provided a list which includes some popular symbolic associations that align with each keyword, to help you find inspiration when it comes to finding the right pieces for your kit. Feel free to copy the sets I list throughout these books as examples if you would prefer to start off with one which is tried and tested.

- Love
- Relationships
- Friendships
- Self-love
- Health
- Wealth
- Career
- Selflessness
- Travel
- Communication
- Creativity
- Warning
- Burn out (as in, you are taking too much on and risking burn-out)
- Happiness
- Spirituality
- Home Life
- Fear
- Taking a risk
- Intuition
- Beware

Out of the list of keywords above, can you see any that could be easily combined? I personally think that love, relationships, friendships, and self-love could be combined. Self-love and selflessness also have the potential to work well under one stone, as could beware, taking a risk, and maybe even intuition. Have a go at writing your own list, playing around with the different meanings and seeing how different combinations work for you. If you would much rather prefer having just one keyword for each stone, then stick with that for the time being.

Now that you have your keywords you can start to look at

expanding their meanings into messages. As I said, keywords are great, but they can be restrictive. When we perform our reading we essentially read the stones like a story based on how they relate to one another. Adding more breadth and depth to the meanings behind your stones will make this much easier.

One thing I have learned is that the more you use your stones, the more they will talk to you. You will find that a stone that represents health for example could mean physical health in one reading, mental health in another, or even financial help in another if it lands next to a stone that represents money. In one reading it may represent needing to take a step back and recuperate to improve your health, in another it may represent being more active to improve your health. The meanings and messages you assign should be used as a guideline in your reading to point you in the right direction. It is your intuition which will help you understand the particular meaning of a specific stone in the context of your reading.

Your messages don't need to be paragraphs and paragraphs of in-depth analysis. Especially when starting out, just two or three sentences will do. You may find that these change over time as you practice and get to know your stones better. Think of these meanings and messages as something fluid rather than fixed, and remember to keep them relevant to your original keyword. Below is a real top-level look at the messages of each stone in my own general lithomancy set to help get you started. You can also take a look at the planetary correspondence associations for inspiration.

**Onyx:**
**Keyword:** Protection
**Meaning:** In this set, Onyx represents protection. There is something bubbling under the surface that you should be wary of. This could be something unexpected, or it may be something that you are aware of but may be underestimating. Be careful,

cautious, and take steps to protect yourself as you progress.

## Tiger's Eye:

**Keyword:** Opportunity

**Meaning:** Here, Tiger's Eye represents opportunity. Fortune is smiling on you, and you either have been or will be presented with a great opportunity. It may be an opportunity you are uncertain as to whether to take, but this stone tells you that fate is on your side. Be brave, be bold, and go for it.

## Green Aventurine:

**Keywords:** Relationships, Health

**Meaning:** In this set, Green Aventurine has two different meanings; it represents health, as well as fostering positive relationships and ties. It is telling you that you need to reach out and build relationships with other people if you want to succeed. It may not be friendships; it may even just be networking at events for work purposes for example. Or, possibly, health issues could be at the fore. Whilst I caution against adding two unrelated keywords to a stone, I have learned that my intuition is pretty good in helping me easily determine which one is relevant to the reading.

## Moonstone:

**Keywords:** Femininity, self-care

**Meaning:** The purpose of the Moonstone in this set is to represent the divine feminine and self-love. There is a feminine influence guiding you (which could even be yourself) and you should embrace it. It is time to focus on you, what is best or most important to you, and prioritize that for now.

## Blue Lace Agate:

**Keywords:** Communication, creativity

**Meaning:** In this set Blue Lace Agate represents communication and creative expression. There may be a need to work on your communication skills; do you feel like no-one is listening to you, or you aren't able to get your points across? Focus on improving your own communication style and how you communicate with others to succeed. Don't be afraid to be you. Use your voice to communicate out to the world what you want to help you get ahead and achieve your visions, especially your creative visions.

**Amethyst:**
**Keyword:** Intuition
**Meaning:** Amethyst in this set represents trusting your intuition. Whatever situation you find yourself in, you need to look at the bigger picture and not just the immediate. There may be something you are missing, and if there is then your intuition will guide you to the best resolution. Trust in yourself to make the right decision either way, but make sure you have all of the information available to you before you make that decision.

**Sea Glass:**
**Keywords:** Joy, travel
**Meaning:** The Sea Glass represents an unexpected message of joy, some happiness that will soon come your way. So, if you find yourself going through a difficult period then hold on – things will get better. It can also represent travel, although I have found not that often in my readings.

**Coin:**
**Keyword:** Abundance
**Meaning:** In this set the Coin (unsurprisingly) represents abundance and prosperity. It may not necessarily be financially, but it will most likely be something rooted in the physical world. For example, if your business is struggling because you can't afford to pay your staff for all of the hours you need, then it may manifest in someone offering to do some volunteer work for you

as opposed to you receiving more money. It can also represent your career, and progress and success (or lack of).

**Shell:**
**Keyword:** Emotions
**Meaning:** I have a small Shell in this set which represents the emotional state, especially emotional freedom. You may be, or will have to, deal with a loss. It is time to accept it and let it go if you want to move forward.

**Pebble:**
**Keyword:** Selflessness
**Meaning:** The Pebble represents selflessness, and working on your priorities to build a stable foundation from which to progress from. It may be time to give more of yourself and find happiness or a purpose in helping others.

**Pebble with Arrow:**
**Keyword:** Masculinity
**Meaning:** This is a Pebble with an arrow drawn on it, and it represents energy, vitality and a masculine influence. You are filled with enthusiasm and positivity, and this is a great time to put that to good use and focus on your goal. It could also represent 'someone else' who is going to be an important influence in your life, for better or worse.

## Planetary Correspondences

If you are using the traditional planetary correspondences for your set, then you will need thirteen stones in total. Seven stones represent different planetary influences – the Sun, the Moon, Mars, Venus, Mercury, Jupiter and Saturn. The remaining six represent place, love, magic, life, luck, and commitment. If you are going for the more modern version, then you will need an additional three planetary stones to represent Uranus,

Neptune and Pluto. Below is an overview as to what each of these represent. There are some resources I have seen where each stone has a chapter's worth of associations for each stone. Whilst I'm not going to go into that much depth, this should provide you with a decent overview of each correspondence and the associations it will have for your stone to get started with.

## The Sun:

**Keywords:** Masculinity, energy, purpose, success, leadership, potential, identity, egotism, selfishness, arrogance

**Meaning:** The Sun is associated with masculinity, our personal energy, our needs and our life's purpose. It represents us in our most physical sense, what we want out of life, and how we get it. It talks of achieving our personal goals and finding success, recognition and respect through our hard work. It teaches us not to give up, to be a leader and take control to overcome obstacles and setbacks as we set out to uncover our full potential.

The sun stone represents our sense of identity and individualism. It focuses on how we present ourselves to the outside world and the people around us, and our creative expression. We have the desire to make our mark on the world, and can charm others into believing in our vision with ease.

In business, it can symbolize taking action and dealing with challenges as soon as they arise. Strategy is important in helping you succeed, as is acknowledging that sometimes it just doesn't work out no matter how hard you try. Take these failures as a learning experience and move on. In all areas of life, it emphasizes honesty, self-control, loyalty and keeping one's word. There is also a negative side to the power of the sun. It can also symbolize egotism, selfishness, acting rashly and arrogance.

## The Moon:

**Keywords**: Femininity, emotions, relationships, memories, the home, motherhood, cycles, anxiety, fickleness, forgetfulness

**Meaning:** Whereas the sun represents masculinity, the moon represents femininity. It is tied to all things related to our emotions and our emotional selves. It emphasizes the need to be emotionally balanced and find stability and security in our emotional state. Humans experience a wide range of feelings, from love, to jealousy or anger, and the moon governs them all. It can also influence how we interact with others and present ourselves in our relationships.

Memories and personal experience are important, and not just the positive ones. Sometimes emotional instability can arise from previous traumas and the moon represents the inner light needed to overcome them.

The moon also represents the home, motherhood and nurturing those around you, compassion and understanding. It can help us employ intelligent thinking and planning when dealing with issues, especially when they are related to domestic and economic situations.

As the moon waxes and wanes through its phases, it also represents the flow and the cycles of life. The moon has many faces and this can be representative of ourselves, and the sometimes fickle nature of our wants, needs, and beliefs. There is also a negative side to the moon's energy. It can symbolize moodiness, anxiety, an inability to act without others approval or input, unreliability, forgetfulness and fickleness.

**Mars:**

**Keywords:** Individuality, assertiveness, ambition, dominance, survival, sexual appetite, passion, aggressiveness, selfishness

**Meaning:** Mars is traditionally known as the planet of war. In a sense it is quite similar to the sun. However, where the sun is focused on us as individuals and how we present ourselves to the external world, mars energy has more of a brash, selfish and self-centred streak to it. Our relationships with others under the sun are usually harmonious, mutually beneficial and friendly.

Under Mars there is less concern for others and a lot more for achieving what we want regardless of others.

Mars represents assertiveness, dominance, our desires and ambition. Again like the sun, it is very physical, and our determination and will to succeed is often demonstrated through action. Sexual appetite, our survival instinct, and other primeval drives are governed by Mars.

Mars energy is strong and will power through no matter what. People working with Mars energy usually succeed, being both bold and fearless and never letting anything keep them down. Full of passion, they will fight for and defend what they believe in.

These traits can be extremely positive when applied consciously and with care and consideration for others. It is this lack of consciousness and care that can be an issue when under the influence of Mars. There is a tendency to act without thinking, and to act rashly or aggressively. Success may come at the expense of others.

**Venus:**
**Keywords:** Love, beauty, comfort, socialness, diplomacy, charm, luxury, fulfilment, the arts, vanity, greediness
**Meaning:** Venus is well known as the planet of love, beauty, and the arts. It represents peace, harmony, happiness, comfort, and living our lives in the pursuit of such.

It has a strong influence on social situations and radiates charm, magnetism, graciousness, humor, and cooperation. Venus emphasizes sharing our happiness with others, how we project ourselves, and interact with others. Diplomacy and creating an environment where everyone can come together and feel comfortable is what this energy strives for.

Venus speaks to us of luxury, sensuality, and self-fulfilment, focusing on quality not quantity. It helps soften and ride the waves of life, sure of ourselves and our place in the world with genuine love in our hearts. It can help us channel all of the above into artistic pursuits.

As with all of the signs there are also negative traits associated with Venus. One can become enamored with physical pleasures and be prone to vanity and greediness. When giving so much of themselves to others it can be easy to become offended if it is not appreciated or reciprocated.

## Mercury:
**Keywords:** Communication, the mind, rationalisation, intelligence, wit, disdain, judgement

**Meaning:** The main associations of Mercury are communication and intelligence. It represents the conscious mind and logical thinking. Often those under Mercury energy will feel the need to rationalize everything around them and are very information orientated.

This sort of intelligent thinking is related to communication as it influences the way that we express ourselves. Ideas are often communicated using facts, evidence, and logic. It is a great mediator and can help bridge the divide and encourage compromise that works for all parties. Mercury governs communication even down to how we intone certain words and the vocabulary we use.

Mercury can help us attune to our mental awareness and how the world around us influences our thoughts and mental faculties. Perceptive, quickness, intelligence and wit are often associated with those under Mercury energy, and these people know how to use communication to gain a favorable outcome.

Of course there are downsides to Mercury. Whilst rational and logical thinking can serve us in many ways, it can make it difficult to engage with and communicate emotional needs and wants. When encountering those who think emotionally or not as rationally as themselves, those influenced by Mercury can become disdainful or judgemental of others.

**Jupiter:**
**Keywords:** Luck, abundance, opportunity, optimism, ideologies, benevolence, justice, travel, extravagance, entitlement
**Meaning:** Jupiter is known as a planet of luck, abundance, opportunity, and success. Even during the most challenging of times Jupiter can bring us optimism and promise us that better times are on the horizon. It encourages growth and teaches us that even the most difficult of paths can lead to great opportunities, so long as we keep walking it with hope in our hearts. The positivity of Jupiter is infectious and this good fortune and success can spread to every aspect of our lives by helping us be open to the opportunities we are presented with.

Jupiter is also seen as representing the higher mind. It can broaden our awareness and help us expand our beliefs and knowledge in all areas of life. It encourages us to explore our own thoughts, feelings, and ideologies, and is therefore quite philosophical in this sense. It can help us see the bigger picture and where we fit in and find a deeper significance in the world around us.

The benevolent nature of Jupiter represents justice, truth, and fairness, and also helps us strive to live by our principles. It also represents travel. The negative aspects of Jupiter include extravagance, self-righteousness, and a belief that one is entitled to everything they have been blessed with. It can also encourage complacency or procrastination when someone is used to everything coming so easily to them.

**Saturn:**
**Keywords:** Lesson learned, experience, perseverance, challenges, commitment, responsibility, pessimism, burdens
**Meaning:** Saturn is often seen as a negative influence over people's lives. However, Saturn is a teacher. We all experience setbacks and find ourselves in difficult situations, but what matters is how we react to them and learn from them. Saturn

teaches us that we can take these difficulties, reflect on them, and use them to make more informed decisions later on. By learning from our mistakes we are more likely to succeed the next time. This approach can help us build solid foundations, develop good habits, and be better prepared to handle any challenges we face along the way.

Saturn encourages us to master our skills and to reflect on how we conduct ourselves to make sure that we work smarter, not harder. Whilst challenging, these lessons can teach us knowledge, wisdom, and perseverance.

Structure is also emphasized by Saturn which is not always a bad thing. In fact, structure can be very beneficial in our lives. Commitment, responsibility, and duty are all ruled by Saturn.

However, when taken to extremes it is easy for these positives to turn into negatives. Those influenced by Saturn energy have the ability to become pessimistic and revel in their misery rather than focus on the lessons they could be learning. As such they tend to ignore them and so carry on making the same mistakes over and over again. Too much structure can be limiting, and it can be easy to feel burdened by the duties and responsibilities we have.

**Uranus:**
**Keywords:** Change, reform, innovation, radicalisation, creativity, transformation, rebelliousness
**Meaning:** Uranus can represent sudden or unexpected change. This can be liberating or chaotic, and oftentimes it is up to you to determine whether this change is a positive or negative one. It can symbolize a change in direction, new opportunities and a chance for reform and innovation.

Uranus can also represent freedom from the norm and the breaking down of mundane restrictions and limitations, which can allow us to flourish. This can be especially true in a creative sense.

It allows us to evolve and transform, which can aid us in self-discovery, individuality, and encourage productivity. However, this change could also be unpredictable and difficult to navigate. There is definitely a rebellious streak to Uranus energy and you should be careful not to get too caught up in the moment without carefully considering the potential consequences of your actions.

**Neptune:**

**Keywords:** Mystery, spirituality, other worlds, connection, illusion

**Meaning:** Neptune is seen as a planet of mystery and all things other-worldly. It can represent our intuition and all aspects of our spirituality. Our subconscious mind is governed by Neptune, and so this planet can help us determine what is going on beneath the surface. It can represent our deepest desires, fantasies, and hopes and fears. A planet which is associated with the sea, Neptune also promotes a deep connectivity with the world around us and the world within us.

One of the main aspects of Neptune is its association with illusion. Perhaps not all is as it seems, or maybe you are deliberately avoiding the reality of a situation. Or perhaps you are living in a fantasy world of your own design and as such are unable to deal with the situation at hand. Neptune tells us it is time to break through these illusions. Whilst retreating into our own little fantasy worlds can be a fun form of escapism, if we spend too much time there then our real world will suffer. It tells us to beware of deception. However, it can also encourage us to look outside the box and view situations through new eyes.

**Pluto:**

**Keywords:** The unseen, the unknown, transformation, shadow selves

**Meaning:** For the purposes of lithomancy, yes, Pluto is defined as a planet. Pluto represents the unseen or those little things which build up, until eventually they crash down upon us. 'The straw that broke the camel's back' is a phrase which comes to mind when we talk about Pluto.

It is a planet associated with transformation. although this transformation is often long and not exactly easy. However difficult this change is, sometimes it is necessary to be able to move on and start anew. It is both creation and destruction for you can't have one without the other.

Pluto also encourages us to seek and explore the unknown. This could be on a personal level, or in a wider context such as the mysteries of death and the universe. It can force us to take a look at our 'shadow selves', those things that we keep secret or hidden, and to face them and work on them. Whilst Pluto may be seen as a negative influence, all of this can be extremely beneficial to our lives and should be embraced rather than feared.

**The Place Stone:**
**Keywords:** Home, external environment
**Meaning:** This stone can represent any place with special significance to the reader. This could be work, a place of worship, etc. It essentially represents our physical environment and our relationship to it. Our environment is extremely important; it can provide safety, shelter, and a place to relax and recuperate. We may reside there with family or friends, or alone. The home can also be a source of practicality and can affect us financially as well as physically and mentally. This stone can provide us with information about how our external environment is affecting us or how it will affect us.

**The Love Stone:**
**Keywords:** Love, relationships, self-love
**Meaning:** The love stone represents our loved ones, our relationships, and anyone that we have any sort of emotional connection with such as work colleagues. It also represents self-

love and the way in which we feel towards our own self. It may not necessarily mean romantic love, but rather our connection with ourselves and others.

## The Magic Stone:

**Keywords:** Time, fate

**Meaning:** The magic stone actually represents time and the flow of progress. It can give us an idea as to when to act, how quickly to act, and what to act on. It can often indicate that all things are unfolding as they should, but as always you should use your intuition to determine if this is the meaning of this stone in the context of your reading.

## The Life Stone:

**Keywords:** Personal outlook, satisfaction

**Meaning:** The life stone represents the reader, and how they feel about themselves and the situation they are reading about. It symbolizes our thoughts, attitudes, beliefs, hopes and fears. It deals with all aspects of our being – physical, mental, emotional, and spiritual. It can indicate satisfaction or dissatisfaction with a particular situation, inspire us into action or serve as a warning.

## The Luck Stone:

**Keywords**: Fortune, pay off

**Meaning:** The luck stone represents good fortune. This doesn't necessarily mean a lucky or unexpected break. This luck could come as a direct result of the work the reader is putting into their endeavours and show that a positive outcome is favored. It is a signal that you are on the right track and are making good progress towards your goals.

## The Commitment Stone:

**Keywords:** Commitment, discipline, practicality

**Meaning:** The commitment stone encompasses a broad range of various aspects that make up commitment. These include our own will, self-discipline, time management, energy, and even practical considerations such as how far one might have to drive to reach an appointment being a factor in your commitment to something. It often encourages us to look at all aspects of a situation before we commit and to be sure of what we are committing to. The commitment itself is again broad; it could be towards something personal such as giving up a bad habit, to a new contract or relationship.

It may feel like there is a lot of information to take in when we talk of the planetary influences but this really is just the tip of the iceberg when it comes to the astrological associations assigned in lithomancy. There are many good resources out there which go into much more detail if you are looking for additional information on them.

## Empowering Your Stones with their Meanings

The next step is to actually imbue your stones with the energy of their particular message, the intent. If you are planning on decorating your stones and haven't done so then this is the perfect time to do it. As you decorate, keep your keywords and messages in mind as this will help strengthen your intent.

If you are using the planetary correspondences as meanings for your stones, you will still need to perform this step if you are creating your own set. In fact, even if you have bought a pre-made set then there is no harm in following the steps to empower your stones and help you forge a connection with them. It is this connection which will ultimately strengthen your readings and aid your intuition in interpreting them.

I personally believe the best way to imbue your stones with their meaning is through meditation. It does not have to be for long, even five or ten minutes will make a difference. I also recommend taking a short break before each stone to help clear your mind and make sure you don't tire yourself out.

Find somewhere comfortable where you won't be disturbed and hold the stone in your hands. Focus on transferring your intent and the association into it. Take the association of love; as you hold the stone, focus on love and the message you want the stone to bring you. How does the energy of 'love' feel to you? For me it is warm, happy and comforting. Focus on pouring this from yourself and out into your stone. What about an association like your career? For me that is strength, ambition, and satisfaction with achievement.

Each meaning or message has a particular 'energy' you will associate with it, and this is what you will need to imbue into your stones.

You may wish to verbally state your intention to the stone, such as:

> this shell represents my emotional state, especially emotional freedom. It represents that I am, or will have to, deal with a loss. This shell means it is time to accept it and let it go if I want to move forward.

You may find that when you are meditating with your stone that you get the impression of a completely different meaning coming through. For example, you may wish for a piece of Tiger's Eye to represent protection. However, as you meditate with it the word 'courage' pops into your head and the energy you feel from it evokes courage more than it does protection. If this happens then just roll with it! This is a good sign – it shows that you are already becoming tuned to your stones and listening to the messages they are giving you. It may be that you need to find some additional stones to represent the meaning you originally intended, but ultimately trust your intuition and listen to what the stones are telling you.

## Storing Your Stones

I have often heard that divination tools should be kept under a dark cover to protect them, but I have personally never found the need to do this with my lithomancy sets. You could keep them in a pouch or a box if you would prefer. However you decide to store them I absolutely recommend it best to keep them away from prying eyes and wandering fingers! Like all things, your stones have the ability to pick up the energies around them, so it is good practice to keep them stored out of harm's way.

## Upkeep and Maintenance

How often you use your stones will determine how much maintenance and upkeep they need. It is up to you how often, if at all, you cleanse your stones. I personally haven't felt the need to cleanse mine. If you perform readings for other people and you have that other person handling your stones then I would recommend cleansing them immediately after the reading. If at any point you are handling them and are feeling out of sorts – physically ill, or experiencing negative emotions like anger for example – then I would also recommend cleansing them before using them again. It is never recommended that you do any sort of magic or divination when you are feeling ill or in a negative mind frame, but sometimes we go ahead without thinking or realising how we have been affected by what we are feeling. To make sure that none of that negativity has affected your stones, cleanse them just in case.

The more regularly you use your stones, the easier it will be to attune yourself to the energies of them when performing a reading. However, if you don't use them often, or you go a long period without using them then you may find it useful to meditate with each one and their associations on a more regular basis to make sure you don't lose your connection with them.

## Chapter 3

# Preparing for a Reading

Your preparations can be as simple or as elaborate as you wish. If you are new to lithomancy or divination as a whole then putting some effort into preparation can help connect you to the higher realm, and open yourself up to receive the messages that are sent to you through the stones.

Once you become more experienced with lithomancy you may wish to dispense with some of the formalities. These days my pre-reading prep is pretty minimal; I will ground, centre, ask for blessings upon my reading with a quick prayer, and then get going. The amount of effort or ritual you want to put into pre-reading preparations is completely up to you. As always, it's down to what feels right for you. Below are some ideas you might want to try to help you get in the right mind set for performing a reading.

### Using Herbs and Scents

- Drink a tea which contains herbs that are known to help to open your third eye or are associated with divination. My personal go-to is anything with dandelion in.
- Make a herbal sachet and keep it on you whilst your perform your reading.
- Add herbs associated with divination to your bath and soak up their energies as you bathe before a reading.
- Burn an incense with a scent associated with divination. You can buy pre-made, or even make your own loose incense blend.
- Anoint yourself with divination oil; you could buy pre-made oil, or you can make your own by adding some of the herbs below into a small glass jar and filling with

a carrier oil such as olive oil, jojoba oil, coconut oil, sweet almond oil, or grapeseed oil. Leave it in a warm environment (such as on a windowsill) for a week or two.

Herbs, flowers, and trees associated with divination and increasing your psychic abilities include ash, beech, dandelion root, mugwort, orange flowers or orange peel, star anise, yarrow, lavender, sage, camphor, jasmine, clove, bay, honeysuckle, and thyme.

Before ingesting or applying any sort of herbal mixture to your skin, do your research and check with a medical professional if you are unsure, or have any pre-existing conditions. Not all herbs are suitable for congestion or should be put in contact with the skin. Some can interfere with medications and some are not suitable for those who are pregnant, so always better to be safe than sorry.

## Using Crystals

- Carry a crystal or two on you as you do your reading.
- Create gem water by leaving one of the crystals below in water overnight (preferably in the light of the full moon if the timing is right), and then drinking it before you do your reading or using it to make tea. Be careful though; some crystals can be damaged if left in water, and can even be toxic. Please research the crystals you wish to use beforehand, or talk to a medical professional.
- Create a crystal grid and meditate with it before you do your reading. You could keep it up whilst you do your reading, or if you have enough crystals, do your reading within a crystal circle. Some practitioners prefer to do their reading within a boundary, usually made out of cord, and throw the stones within this.

Crystals that are associated with divination and increasing your psychic abilities include lapis lazuli, calcite, clear quartz (clear quartz is a crystal which is great at amplifying the energies around it, so is good to use in conjunction with other crystals in this list), amethyst, selenite, fluorite, labradorite, herkimer diamond, moonstone, obsidian, tiger's eye, opal, and emerald.

## Using Colour Magic

- Light a silver or purple candle, both colours associated with divination and fortune telling.
- Wear a cord of either purple or silver, or both colours intertwined.
- Wear an item of clothing, such as a scarf in one these colours, that you save especially for performing readings.

## Cleansing Your Space

Cleansing your space of negative energies will help create a positive place for you to conduct your readings in. Below are some quick and easy ways of cleansing the space:

- Use the smoke of the incense such as sage, and walk clockwise around your space with it, wafting the smoke as you go so it reaches every corner of the room.
- Walk in a clockwise circle around your space and sprinkle salt as you go.
- Grab a broom and sweep your space, again in a clockwise direction.

## Other Ideas for Preparation:

- Put on some soothing or meditative music.
- Develop a trigger. Triggers are great for helping you quickly get into the right mind set. If you perform a certain action, or say a particular phrase, every time you prepare for a reading, then eventually just performing that action or saying that phrase will be enough to

prepare you. I personally repeat the phrase *as the river flows, let me mind be open to the sea* three times in my head before performing lithomancy. Your trigger may even be something physical, such as wearing a specific piece of jewellery or a scarf when you perform readings. Or it may be audible, such as listening to a specific playlist. Whatever your trigger is, make sure you perform it every time you are preparing to do a reading.

The bare minimum is to make sure that you won't be bothered by any distractions. Choose a time when you can guarantee you won't be interrupted by people you live with or visitors, and turn off your phone. Make sure that you are comfortable; think about the temperature of the room, the clothing you are wearing, the amount of noise (such as from traffic – I live near a fire station so sirens are a common occurrence when I'm trying to focus).

Think about the dimensions of the space that you are casting in and the effect it will have on your stones. A thickly carpeted floor gives the stones less room to roll and 'move around', whilst a hard floor could damage your stones. I have a small prayer mat that I use on a hardwood floor for readings which protects the stones but also gives them space to move around.

Make sure you are not in so small a space that your stones could get lost under furniture. Some people like to cast their stones into a box or similar to ensure they don't bounce around and get lost. Whilst this is a good idea if you are limited on space, but it can also restrict the reading and isn't ideal.

Experiment with the different ways in which you can prepare for your reading and see if you can find one which works for you. Everyone is different; whilst I find music helps me focus, others might find it distracting. Try to incorporate some level of preparation into your practice, no matter how small.

# Chapter 4

# Performing a Reading

Now we are ready to perform our reading! We have a fair bit to cover in this section but it should be relatively straight forward. We will look at how to cast your stones, how to perform a yes/no reading, and how to perform readings for others. We will also approach the issue 'to read within a boundary or not', and with or without segments, as well as ideas for segmentation (I will explain what all of this means later on).

Most of this chapter will be dedicated to interpreting your stones and how to do so. There are quite a few different elements you can look at to help you interpret your reading, as well as some classic patterns to keep an eye out for.

All of the below is relevant whether you are using a pre-made set which you have bought online, a set you have made yourself, or if you are using a set with associations already outlined such as the planetary correspondences.

## Casting Your Stones

Despite some of the terminology we may use, never, ever, throw your stones! If you launch your stones across the room you could break them, lose them, and end up with stones so far removed from one another that being able to interpret them is impossible.

Instead, you can either simply hold your stones between you two hands and then drop them onto the surface you will be reading on, or you can try tossing them very gently out in front of you.

Before you cast, take a few moments to ground and centre and hold your stones between your cupped hands. I like to move them around in my hands (not quite shaking them) whilst focusing on my question. Trust that divine energies are watching over you and your stones will give you the most accurate reading possible. Whisper you question out loud to your stones and when you feel ready, cast them as described above.

It sounds simple but even casting can take a little bit of practice. Working out the best height to cast them from, or how far in front of you to cast them are all things you will learn as you go. You may find on your first couple of tries that you launch your stones too far across the room, or maybe not far enough and they all fall into your lap. See if there are enough that have fallen conveniently to be able to do your reading and if not, try again.

## Yes or No Readings

I thought we would take a quick look at performing yes/no readings first as these are the most simple to get to grips with. Follow the guidelines above to cast your stones whilst focusing on your question.

If you are using a personal stone then the yes/no stone which falls closest to it will provide you with your answer. If you aren't using a personal stone then whichever stone falls closest to you will be your answer.

It sounds very straight forward but you can get more out of your reading than just yes or no, even with just two or three stones. In the *interpreting your stones* section we will be taking a look at how distance, location, and special features of your stones can be used to infer additional detail from your reading. This will also be relevant for the yes/no readings so make sure you check it out.

## Reading Within a Boundary

When we talk about using a circle or a boundary in our lithomancy readings, we don't mean a magic or protective circle as you might cast when performing a ritual. Rather, we mean a circle marked on the floor, usually by a cord that you cast the stones into. 'Reading within a circle' has a much better ring to it than 'reading within a boundary', but the last thing I want to do is cause confusion. So I will stick with calling it a boundary.

This boundary serves two purposes; first, it can provide a focus as to which stones you should include in your reading. Generally, any stones which land outside of the boundary are discarded and it is only those within the circle that are used in your interpretation. However, as with all things in lithomancy you should listen to your intuition. Sometimes stones may fall just outside of the boundary or even on the boundary line itself, and your intuition could tell you that these are still relevant. If this is the case then it could symbolize one of three things:

- That this element is currently in play but hidden from the reader and could emerge in the future.
- That this element is not currently in play but could arise in the future.
- That this element is not of immediate importance, but should be something the reader keeps an eye on moving forward.

The second reason for using a boundary is that you can use this circle to split your reading into segments such as periods of time, or different aspects of your life for example. This is the segmentation I mentioned above and I will go into a bit more detail about it shortly.

Essentially we have three slightly different ways of performing readings; no boundary, within a boundary, or within a segmented boundary. Performing readings with no boundary or within a boundary follow the same methodology when it comes to interpreting your readings. The only difference is that the boundary makes it clearer which stones should and should not be included in the reading. Once we introduce segments it becomes a little different, but the principles of interpretation are still the same.

I personally prefer to work without a boundary and without segments. However, using segments can be a lot of fun, especially if you find a layout that works for you. You can even combine the two. If I am performing a reading for someone else, I will start off by doing a reading without a boundary. Once I have interpreted this I will perform another short reading by casting onto a segmented grid split into different aspects (such as money, health, love, etc.). This can help me see if I have missed anything or misinterpreted anything in the main reading.

That's pretty much all there is to a boundary; whether you use one or not, the way you interpret the stones will still be the same.

## Reading with Segments

Segments can be extremely useful, and also give us a chance to be a bit creative with our readings. A segmented circle can be used to help define different time periods depending on how far into the future you want to perform your reading, different elements specific to your reading, or you could even incorporate the astrological houses.

You don't need to mark these out physically if you don't want to but it does help. Simply get some cord or string and mark out a circle split into the relevant number of segments onto whatever surface you will be reading on. I find it virtually impossible to make a perfect shaped circle when it comes to using cord so don't worry if it is a bit misshapen! The most important aspect is trying to make sure that the segments you have created are all roughly the same size.

Let's say I want to do a reading to tell me what is going to happen over the next year. I could divide my circle into twelve segments, as below:

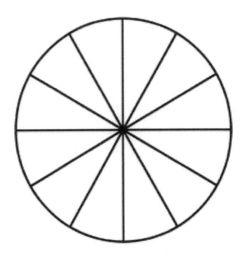

Each segment would then represent a month, and you would interpret your reading based on which stones fell within which segments. For example, if your stone representing health fell in the segment assigned to January, then it is indicative of health issues being at the fore during January. If the stone were to fall on the line that separates January and February then it would be safe to assume that health will feature in both January and February.

If any of the stones fall in the centre of the circle, this is a good indicator that the association of that stone (money, career, using your intuition, etc.,) will be one you need to factor into your life throughout the whole year.

Does it matter where in the segments the stones fall? Sometimes it does. The closer to the centre of the circle the stones fall, the more prominent their influences are in the reading or the quicker they will manifest. Stones which fall closer to the outside of the segment will likely be either less important or slower to manifest. Stones that fall outside of the boundary completely can either be taken out of the reading, or they may represent something hidden, something coming up, or something the reader should keep an eye on. However, this is not a hard and fast rule. I have performed readings using segments where my intuition has told me that exactly where the stones fell in the segment wasn't of too much importance. As always, trust your gut.

If you are using the above method then you do not need to include your personal stone in the reading if you use one.

As with the yes/no readings, there is still more you can look for to help you interpret your reading. In the *interpreting your stones* section we will be taking a look at how distance and any 'special features' of your stones can be used to infer additional detail from your reading, which will also be relevant to those performing readings with segments.

You can split your circle up however you want, and to represent whatever you want so long as you keep the segments of equal size and shape. Below are some more ideas to get you started but feel free to come up with your own and see how they work for you.

- Split into four equal segments, each representing one of the four seasons (spring, summer, autumn/fall, winter).
- Perform a reading representing a month's overview, with the circle segmented depending on whether there are four or five weeks in the month.
- Split it into three equal segments to represent the past, present, and future.
- Split into twelve equal segments to represent the twelve astrological houses.

You can also use this method to split your circle into different elements associated with your overall query. Let's say that you are planning on going backpacking and visiting six different countries. You could split the circle into six different segments, each representing a country on your trip, and use a lithomancy reading to inform you as to how each portion of your trip could play out. Or maybe you are just starting a new job and want to know how it will affect different aspects of your life? You could split the circle into segments representing finances, health, family, love, etc., and read these influences in relation to your career change.

Using a piece of cord to create the circle in front of you is quick and flexible. However, if you want something a bit more permanent, you can always create one out of card or even paper. I have one I made out of a circular piece of paper in which I have drawn equal sized segments and assigned one to each of the below:

Love
Career
Spirituality
Health
Wealth
Relationships
Dangers
Ego Self

This is what I cast my stones onto to perform a reading when I need something quick and quite high level, and also after performing a more general reading for others to make sure I haven't missed or misinterpreted anything.

## Interpreting Your Reading

We have thought of our question, focused on it, and cast our stones. What happens next? Well, next we need to determine which of the stones are most relevant to the reading, or those issues which will be at the forefront. As I've mentioned a few times now, if you are using a personal stone then it will be the stones which fall closest to this which will be the most relevant. The further away other stones are from it, the less prominent an influence they will be. If you aren't using a personal stone then you will be focusing on where the stones fall in proximity to you. Again, those that fall closest to you will be the most relevant and the stones falling further away representing less prominent influences.

I tend to use a personal stone in my readings so I'm going to carry on discussing the reading as if you had used a personal stone, but remember that this information is just as relevant if you are going by which stones have fallen closest to you.

Not only do we take into account the visual patterns in which the stones have fallen, but we use our intuition to 'listen' to the stone's messages. With lithomancy being so intuitive, each reader will develop their own system of interpretation, and this comes with practice. I will go through some of the most popular patterns but you may find after some practice that the stones talk to you in a completely different way. You may also find that your interpretations differ slightly in each set you use or depending on what questions you ask. When I am using my general lithomancy set I find that most of the stones will feed into the reading in some way. However, depending on the sorts of questions I ask of my sea-themed lithomancy set, sometimes just one or two stones out of the nine I use will be relevant to the reading. My sea-themed set can seem quite 'blunt' and to the point in that regard.

As you can imagine there are almost countless patterns that could crop up in your readings, so this is by no means a comprehensive list, but rather a guide to some of the most common you will encounter.

When interpreting our reading there are five main elements we consider which will help us build up our overall interpretation. These are:

- The distance between stones (or lack of).
- How far away the stones fall from your personal stone or where they fall in relation to the boundary edge if you

are using one.

- The physical patterns the stones create as they fall (such as square shapes, circular shapes, straight lines, etc.).
- The stones physical characteristics (such as any points it has, rough or smooth sides, etc.), and any other influences such as light/shadow.
- How the meanings and messages of the stones interact with and influence each other.

## Distance

The distance between your stones can give you an idea as to how strongly connected the messages or influences of the stones are, or the speed at which things may manifest.

First take a look at your reading as a whole. Are there lots of little clusters, or are the stones more evenly spread out? Lots of little clusters can represent lots of different, potentially unrelated elements within the reading. The stones being more evenly spaced out can represent a more balanced flow of energy and more general connectivity between the elements at play in the situation you are reading for.

Next look at how far have they have fallen in relation to your personal stone, or from you if you aren't using a personal stone. The further away they are the less prominent their influence, or the slower they may take to manifest. Which one of these two it is, is up to your intuition to decide. If you are using a boundary or segments are any of the stones crossing any segments? Have they fallen close to the centre or are there any which have fallen outside of the boundary that could potentially be discarded?

Occasionally you may get readings where every single stone has fallen a long distance out from the personal stone. This could represent that the querent (the person you are performing the reading for) is quite removed or distanced from everything that is going on, in denial about the situation, or is experiencing a lack of control. It could also indicate that perhaps these influences and messages are still some way off from manifesting in their life, or that there is no clear priority.

Another thing to look out for when it comes to distance is whether more stones have fallen in the bottom half or in the top half. There are many readings I have done, most often with my sea lithomancy or my chakra set, where the personal stone falls in the centre. Some stones fall below it and some fall above it in what is a clear split. To me this often feels very much a divide of the internal and external. The stones at the bottom beneath the personal stone represent my 'internal world' – thoughts, feelings, hopes, fears etc. The stones that fall above my personal stone represent the external world, and how I present myself in it.

Once you have taken a look at the above and considered the reading as a whole, you can start to take a look at the individual stones and their relationships to one another.

If you have noticed clusters of stones within your reading, the tighter the cluster, the stronger an influence the stones in that cluster will have on one another. As such, the more relevant they are to each other. The further away they are, the weaker this connection is (but not obsolete). It can also be read as those in tighter clusters will manifest quicker and those in looser clusters more slowly, but I personally feel that influence is often more relevant than time when I am performing readings. Even in clusters they will most likely have fallen into some sort of shape or pattern. Below are some of the most common ones and what they represent in a reading.

## Interpreting Patterns and Shapes

Patterns and shapes work twofold; first, the actual geometrical shapes that the stones fall in can provide us further insight in our reading. Second, these shapes can tell us more about how the energy and influences of each stone interact with each other. Below I will go through some of the most common patterns and shapes that can appear and what they symbolize.

We will use an example kit when going through the shapes and patterns below to help build an understanding as to how to read and interpret each one. This will be made up of six stones from a 'general reading' kit:

**Stone A:** Represents relationships. This could be any relationship; a relationship you have with another person, the relationship you have to your career or vocation, or a relationship you have with your environment.

**Stone B:** Represents the home and your domestic environment.

**Stone C:** Represents money and physical wealth.

**Stone D:** Represents self-love. This is the need to put yourself first, and do what is best for your own well-being in any given situation.

**Stone E:** Represents health. This could be physical health, mental health, or emotional health. It could also represent the 'health' of a relationship, your career, your savings, etc.

**Stone F:** Represents opportunities, and success through new ventures.

Keep these in mind as we read through the following examples and you should start to see how we can use our intuition to interpret the shapes and patterns that appear in our reading.

## Straight Lines

Stones falling in a straight line usually represent a direct flow of the energy from one to the other. It is the path of least resistance and a strong indicator of events and manifestations happening in a linear fashion. This is especially true of lines which fall either horizontally or vertically. Diagonal lines can often represent that, whilst this linear path exists, it may not be easy to see in the moment how the events that play out are related to one another.

Straight lines could also represent opposition, or being

'caught in the middle'.

Take for example the below:

A —————————— B —————————— C

You could read A in relation to B, and B in relation to C, but you would not read A in direct relation to C; they are connected by B, but not directly related. There is a clear progression here – A leads to B, and B leads to C. Or you could say that A and C are conflicting forces, and B is stuck in the middle.

Let's take our example set and say that stone A represents relationships, stone B represents the home, and stone C represents money. If we are performing a general reading, we could interpret this as building up relationships within your home and family will play a prominent part in the near future (A – B). You may find that you need to put some thought into financial matters concerning your home to improve these relationships or your situation (B – C).

Or it could be interpreted as there are issues with your home (B), and you are caught between the wants and needs of the people living there (A) and the cost implications that come with keeping those inside the home happy (C). As always, your intuition should be able to steer you towards the most likely interpretation.

## Squares

Squares focus on foundations, stability, and what needs to be in place before you can start or progress:

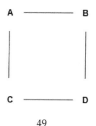

A ——————— B

C ——————— D

This shape, being associated with foundations, represents the need to make sure that you have established stability in the four areas represented above; your relationships, yourself, your home, and your finances. Ask yourself, how is your relationship with money? Your relationships at home and with other people? How do you feel about yourself? Do money worries arise because of your living situation, or do you find money to be an issue that causes friction in your relationships, including the relationship you have with yourself? All of these questions need to be asked and any issues should be dealt with before you take any further action. These energies are all related and so you need to create harmony between them before you progress.

## Triangles

Triangles are similar to squares in a sense. Where the square represents the foundations you need before opportunity can arise, the triangle shows these are already in place. The triangle is more concerned with the opportunity itself, the energies working together to manifest some sort of change, progress, or conclusion.

It represents potential and inspiration and is indicates that whatever is represented here has a good chance of manifesting. However, there is also the implication that the querent needs to put the work in to help it manifest, as if they don't then it may not manifest to its fullest potential:

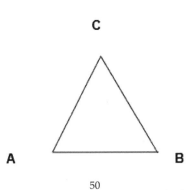

Here we can see the energies of our three stones working together; money to afford the necessary upkeep to a home leads to happy people, which leads to improved relationships. People with good relationships within a home are more likely to care about it and put more of an effort into keeping it tidy, not breaking things, etc. Chances are that things are already going well in your home life and you have a good living situation. However, working on the relationships and financial aspects of home ownership will lead to a great living situation.

## Circles/Curves/Spirals

Circles and spirals represent completeness, wholeness, and harmony. I have found that they don't appear as often as triangles or squares, but when they do, they are a positive sign.

There is a difference between a circle and a cluster. When circles appear in readings, they tend to have a very defined shape – they are very obviously circles; with more than four stones, as opposed to a few stones bunched together. Similar to the straight lines, the energy of each stone flows into the next in a linear fashion. However, the circle/spiral is more subtle, slightly more intertwined, and the flow more harmonious than we encounter with straight lines.

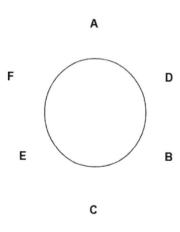

51

Here we could say that our relationships will affect how we feel about ourselves (A – D) and so we should strive to maintain positive relationships which we feel good in. Once we feel happier in ourselves, we will feel happier in our environment (D – B). This in turn will lead us to improve our relationship with money; maybe we will feel motivated to manage any financial issues we are experiencing, or maybe we will realize that relationships are more important than money (B – C).

Getting our financial situation under control will ultimately improve our health – maybe money worries were causing anxiety for example (C – E). When our physical and mental health is good, we feel more energetic and positive, which could attract or open ourselves up to new opportunities (E – F). When we take on new opportunities, we also have the chance to meet new people and form new relationships (F – A), and so the cycle continues.

A curve is somewhere between a straight line and a circle in regards to how it should be interpreted. The linear way of interpreting it is the same, but it is not as complete as the circle, nor is it rigid as the straight line. Depending on which way the curve bends, you may find that the energy throughout this progression isn't consistent. A curve bending upwards could represent a slight uphill struggle, or slow progress, but ultimately it will lead to success. A curve downwards could symbolize an easy run, or that the path will lead to challenges that the querent will need to pull themselves up from to succeed.

Generally I tend to read the stones in a circle or a spiral in a clockwise fashion, but again you will need to use your intuition to determine if this is the best way forward in the reading you are doing.

## Split Paths

I've named this particular pattern 'split paths', because that is exactly what it represents.

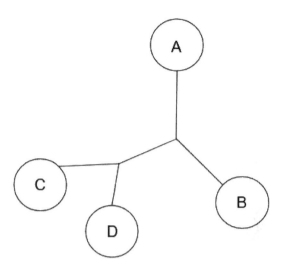

The split path pattern essentially shows us two different paths; it tells us what will happen if we choose one particular path (shown here on the left), and what will happen if we choose a different path (the path splitting off to the right). Sometimes these can be decisive – one path will show what will happen if you take the advice of the stone the paths originate from (in this case stone A), and the other path shows what will happen if you ignore the advice. Other times, there may not be a clear right or wrong path to take and the reader may need to consider further which path would be the best for them.

Below is an example from a reading I did recently where a split path appeared to give you an idea as to how you could interpret this. This is taken straight from my sea-based lithomancy set and so has some different associations for the stones (or in this case, stones and shells):

**Stone A**: In this example stone A is a Mussel Shell. It represents self-discovery. Take a look at your own feelings, biases, and beliefs – even the negative ones such as jealousy – before you proceed. Try to understand, and learn from them before you make a move.

**Stone B**: In this example stone B is a Clam Shell. It represents, peace, love, and harmony; the need to make peace and move on, and forge better and more nurturing relationships.

**Stone C**: In this example stone C is a Limpet Shell. It represents that you are clinging on to something, and you need to decide whether it is worth holding on to, or whether it is time to let it go.

**Stone D**: In this example stone D is a Red Pebble. It represents stopping; something, or someone (it could even be yourself) is working against you, either maliciously or unintentionally.

In this scenario I was asking about a change at work and how I should handle this change. To me, the mussel shell (A) represents that if I'm not happy with the change then I need to first take a look at my own biases and preconceived ideas, and whether the change really is bad or whether I am resisting it.

Then the split comes into play. To the right we have the clam shell (B). To me, this represents what will happen if I take this advice, if I take a look at my own attitude and try to improve it. I will be able to make peace with the changes which have occurred, and I should look at forging new relationships with colleagues to help me adapt to, and support me in, these changes.

To the left we have the limpet shell (C) first. This represents what will happen if I ignore this advice and don't reflect on my own attitude and prejudices – I will be clinging onto something which is not viable anymore. The red pebble (D) just below it signifies that if I keep clinging onto this which does not work anymore, I will only be working against and sabotaging myself.

Above I have given the example of two stones (the red pebble and the limpet shell) opposite one another, and how they work together to give an interpretation. However, sometimes stones which oppose each other can signify conflict so look out and use your intuition to judge which is the correct interpretation.

# A Final Note on Shapes

The shapes in which stones fall can help us by giving us an idea as to how that energy will manifest. Looking at the shapes we have – the straight line, the square, the triangle, and the circle, it might seem difficult to distinguish exactly what the differences are. To break it down:

**Straight lines**: A will lead to B, which will lead to C. It is a quite blunt and very linear progression.

**Squares**: You need to make sure A, B, C and D are working in harmony before you proceed.

**Triangles**: The foundations needed to manifest A, B, and C are already in place. With a bit of extra work, you will achieve success.

**Circles**: A will lead to B, which will lead to C (etc.), and each will move into one another in a harmonious, effortless, free-flowing way.

This is by no means a complete list of the shapes that can appear in your reading. In one reading I gave, the stones fell in a perfect yin yang symbol which gave the impression of two very different flows of energy that worked together in a harmonious fashion. Whilst squares, circles, triangles, lines, and clusters are the most common shapes you will see in every reading, occasionally one which is a bit more unique will pop up. Remember to employ your intuition to determine if any of these shapes are relevant to your reading, and how.

## Interpreting the Stone's Physical Characteristics

It isn't often that you find two stones or two crystals that are exactly the same. Slight discoloration, cracks, and little lumps and bumps all give character to individual stones. These can be used to help you gain further insight into your reading.

I personally recommend that beginners just focus on patterns and distance for now. The best way to discover if any of your stones' little quirks have any symbolism within your reading is to use your intuition to pick these up as you go, rather than assigning them. You may find when you are meditating with your stones that they 'tell' you about any of these characteristics that could indicate something a bit different. However, I have found that again the best way of getting to know what, if any, these are is to use your intuition in the moment, and practice. Things to look out for include (but certainly aren't limited to):

**Points:** Some crystals have natural points, and these can be used in a reading to help determine energy flow. For example, if a pointed crystal appears in a circle or a curve, the point could symbolize whether you should be reading the stones left to right, or right to left, depending on the direction it is pointing. Crystals with points facing down could represent a dip or a slowing of energy and a bit more of a challenge for the reader, whereas points facing upwards could represent unblocked and rapid progress.

**Rough/smooth edges**: If your stone has one rough side, edge, or patch, as well as one smooth, you can use these in your reading. The stone landing rough side up could represent challenges in that area or difficulties the reader should be aware of. The smooth side could represent that progress will be smooth.

**Cracks:** If your stone has a multitude of cracks on one side and is a lot smoother on the other side then again you could use the cracked side to symbolize difficulties and challenges, and the smooth side to symbolize a smooth progression.

**Designation of any other designs/patterns**: If you have decorated your stones yourself, then these can also be used to help bring additional insight into your readings. A stone which lands with the decoration facing the wrong way could symbolize challenges, as could it landing decoration side down.

**Discoloration**: You can also use any patches of discoloration that your stones have in your reading. If you are using a red crystal, but it has one patch which is more pink than red, this could represent that the issue/influence that stone represents is a minor one. The more bright red on show in the reading, the more prominent that issue/influence could be.

**Lighting/Shadow**: Similar to how discolouration can be used, light and shadow can also be used in your readings. Stones which land mostly in shadow could represent more minor influences, slow progression, or challenges, whilst those which appear more lit could be more positive, more important, or quicker to manifest.

## Finishing Your Reading

You can do more than one reading in a session if you would like. I tend to find I can get into a bit of a roll if I am reading for myself, and oftentimes elements will appear in one reading that I will want to explore a bit further – so I'll do another reading. Make sure you don't tire yourself out if you want to do more than one in a sitting, as it becomes easy to miss signs and messages if we are feeling tired or have been focusing for too long.

No matter whether you are using a boundary, a boundary with segments, or no boundary, I recommend that you record every reading you do so you can come back to it later. Make sure you include the stones you have decided to discard when you record it, as you may look back and realize that you missed something by not including them. This reflection will help you better determine in the future at which point you should disregard certain stones because of the distance they fell from the rest of the stones, or their seeming lack of relationship to any of the other stones in the reading. You may wish to make a quick sketch of the layout or take a photo of it. I definitely recommend a more visual approach rather than writing a description as it makes it much easier to identify if you have indeed missed anything later on.

Make sure you clear up all of your stones. It sounds obvious, but especially if you are using quite a few, it can be easy to forget one or two which could then be trodden on or eaten by a pet. Place them wherever you tend to store them (such in a box or a pouch), and say a little 'thank you' to your stones for assisting you. If you call on any deities or spirits to aid you in your readings then make sure you thank them too.

Once you have done this, just take a few minutes to ground and centre and reflect on the experience. Is there anything you feel like you should have done differently, or anything you might want to try next time? Make sure you make a note of these so you don't forget.

## Reading for Others

Casting and interpreting readings for other people is a lot of fun. Like many things, it can be a bit daunting at first, but practice really does make perfect. As you may have guessed by now, intuition is the key. There may be a particular pattern that appears in all of your readings that means one thing to you but in another person's reading could mean something completely different. Keep an open mind, and trust yourself.

Reading for others is not very different from reading for yourself. Possibly the most challenging aspect of it is remembering that this reading isn't about you, and trying not to project your own situation or experiences into the reading. Always keep an awareness that when reading for others, you are more like a conduit through which the universe speaks to help maintain that impartiality.

Whether you are reading for another person whilst they are physically in the room with you, or whether you are performing a long distance reading, I recommend having a chat with the person you are reading for beforehand. Ask them how they are, what they have been up to, and indulge in a bit of small-talk to help you attune to their energy. Ask them if they want a general reading or if they have a specific question or situation in mind that they need some guidance on. If like me you have several different lithomancy sets, then this will also help you determine which set is best for the job. If they have a specific question or situation they are enquiring about, then you can ask for some basic information – however, try not to pry too deep. Not only may your querent not want to divulge the details, but you also don't want to gain any sort of information that may skew the reading or lead you to being less than impartial.

If the person you are reading for is physically present, you may want to ask them to hold the stones and give them a shake to help attune their energy to the stones to help strengthen the reading. Personally, I prefer to not have other people touch my stones, and work on just attuning myself to their energy without any physical interaction, which has always worked well enough. If you don't want them touching your stones but maybe want them to be more involved in the reading, then you could try having them blow gently on your hands whilst focusing on their question as you hold the stones. Or you could have them touch the surface that you will be casting the stones onto whilst they state their question and ask for guidance from the stones.

Before casting your stones, make sure the person you are reading for knows not to touch anything. I would recommend taking a moment to view the layout and gather your initial impressions before you start interpreting the reading out loud. If you touch on something extremely relevant or that the querent feels strongly about, the querent may accidentally lead you off on a bit of a tangent which can break your focus. Depending on how talkative your querent is, it may be best to ask them to wait until you have done the full interpretation before you let them ask any questions.

Occasionally you may get a querent who, after hearing your interpretation, says that it can't be correct and there was nothing in the reading that was remotely relevant to them. If this is the case then be open to their feedback, but I would recommend avoiding going back and reinterpreting something. If you start doing this then you stop listening to your intuition, and you will start second guessing everything you thought you saw in the reading. Before you know it, none of it will make sense any more, and neither you or your querent will get anything out of the reading.

Remember that sometimes any sort of divination can bring up things that your querent may not like or may be worrying to them. I remember doing a reading for a lady where it became very evident that health issues were going to cause further issues financially, within her relationships, etc. She did not take it well. There is always a dilemma in these scenarios; to tell the full, unadulterated truth, or to omit some things from the reading to avoid upsetting or worrying them. When I am in these situations, it really depends on my querent and what they are happy hearing. Always remember that things could change, and there is always a chance you have misinterpreted something – never say to a querent that everything you are telling them is immutable.

Finally, if I have just done a general reading for them, I will usually get out my lithomancy chart (see the section *reading with segments*) and cast the stones there to see where they land. Often they land in a way which corroborates what I have already seen in the more general reading, but this little check can help you pick up on anything you may have missed or help resolve any conflicts you may have seen in the general reading.

## Example Reading

I thought it might be useful to include an example interpretation from one of the most recent readings that I have done. This will be a reading which I have alluded to above, one in which I use my sea-based lithomancy set to help me determine how I will handle some large changes that were coming up at work.

Question: How will I handle this transition at work into a new role and a new team?

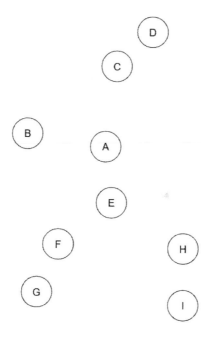

First, let's take a look at the stones as a whole. You can see that they have fallen fairly evenly spaced (mostly done for the purposes of this diagram), and that there are no distinct clusters keeping to themselves. This indicates that there is a good flow of energy, and everything will be relatively linked.

There are three stones which have fallen closest to the personal stone (A), and so these three will be the key 'themes' related to this reading. They are of roughly equal distance from the personal stone, so it would not appear that one is more prominent, or more pressing, than the others. Every stone fell 'right way' up, which is very promising. If there were any which had fallen upside down then we could anticipate difficulties in this area. The mussel shell in this set (E) has a jagged edge, and depending where this points could also indicate difficulties ahead. However, in this reading it fell jagged point away from any of the stones and so will not present any issues. If it had fallen with the jagged edge pointing towards stone H for example, then we could surmise that this path could provide us with some challenges.

In terms of shapes and patterns, this looks fairly straight forward. There are quite a few straight lines and a clear split path from stone E downwards. If we take a closer look, we could piece together some shapes here. G, F, E, H, and it could be considered an arch. A, B, and C could be considered a triangle. However, when I was performing this reading, my gut instinct was that the split path was more prominent than the arch, and that stone B wasn't really connected to anything other than the personal stone. Remember to always follow your first impressions, as this is your intuition guiding you.

Now let's look at the individual stones and how they relate to one another.

**Stone A**: This was my personal stone, and so the stones are read in relation to their proximity to this stone. Now, as I was looking at this spread, the stones, and where they fell, I had a really strong feeling that all of the stones above the personal stone represented the external and how I present myself consciously, and all of the stones underneath represented my internal subconscious. Bear this in mind within the context of this reading.

**Stone B**: This is a piece of Sea Glass and represents trusting that a higher power is watching over you. This tells me that I will be supported throughout this change and to be strong. The fact that this stone fell between the split which defines the external and internal, I felt it was relevant to both aspects. Externally, I will be supported by colleagues and the organisation I work for. Internally, I will have the strength and perseverance to see any challenges through.

**Stone C:** This is a green pebble which represents emotional health and finding balance. This was one of the only stones to fall in the external section of the reading and the closest to the personal stone. As such, I got the impression that this is telling me that this change will be intense and that I need to make sure I'm keeping my emotional health as a priority throughout this period of change.

**Stone D:** This is a cockle shell which represents joy, happiness, new opportunities and doors opening. In the context of this reading I believe it is telling me that this change, if I handle it well, will open new doors and opportunities for me at work and I should make the most of them. It is a very positive sign. However, with the internal and external being so interlinked, I will also need to make sure that I am happy and balanced mentally, emotionally, and spiritually to be able to fully take advantage of these opportunities.

**Stone E:** This is a mussel shell which represents inner reflection, taking a look at our own beliefs and biases (especially the negative ones), understanding them and dealing with them before progressing. This leads me to believe that when things get tough or feel like they aren't working (which often happens with change) I will need to reflect and determine whether these things really aren't working, or whether I am just being resistant to change and looking for fault where there isn't any.

**Stones F and H**: As I mentioned above in the 'split path' patterns section, my intuition told me that these two stones represent two paths; what will happen if I reflect on my own attitude towards change, and what will happen if I continue to resist it. Stone F is a limpet shell. This represents the need to let go of that which doesn't serve me anymore, which in this context could be old ways of working that are no longer relevant thanks to the changes being made.

Stone H is a clam shell which represents making peace and moving on, and forging new relationships. This tells me that to succeed in this new role and new ways of working I will need to build new relationships with the relevant people that I may not have worked with before, to allow me to be successful.

**Stone G**: Stone G is a red pebble which lies directly underneath the limpet shell (stone F). The red pebble acts as a warning, that something or someone (maybe even myself) is out to get me, whether intentionally or unintentionally. Within the context of the limpet shell, which is about letting go of that which does not serve, I read this as a warning as to what will happen if I ignore the message of the limpet shell. Ultimately, I will be sabotaging my own progress by refusing to let go of old ways and embracing new ones.

**Stone I**: This is a black pebble which represents being on the path to, or close to, burn out, and the need to take some time out to rest and recuperate. Like the red pebble, I see this as a warning. If I don't listen to the advice of the cockle and decide to go at it alone rather than trying to build up new relationships, then I won't be able to manage it well and will eventually reach burn out.

## Tying it All Together

Essentially this is going to be a big change, and not necessarily an easy one, but there are things I can do to make sure I navigate it successfully. Overall I need to make sure I am prioritising my emotional health. This change could bring some new opportunities and I need to make sure I am in the right place to be able to make the most of them.

Large scale change is rarely easy. Where I feel like something isn't working or I don't agree with some of the changes, I need to take time to reflect inwardly and work out whether I really don't think these new changes will be beneficial, or whether I am just holding onto old ways of working, refusing to let go and generally resisting the changes. If I don't do this and instead try to cling to these old ways, then I will ultimately just be sabotaging myself which will negatively impact my ability to do my work.

Once I have accepted these new ways of working, I will need to start building new relationships with others that I work with (and perhaps haven't worked closely with in the past) to help me succeed in this role. This will be important, for if I try to go at it alone then I will just end up burning out.

## Chapter 5

# The Chakra Stone Set for Healing

I practice energy healing regularly and I started to wonder, can I use lithomancy to help me with energy healing? I was sure that there must be something there so began to play around and experiment with different ideas. What I found was some of the most useful and relevant readings I have ever had within lithomancy. It has worked so well that I can't not share it!

Lithomancy is first and foremost a divination method. This is how it has been traditionally used for centuries. One of the primary uses of divination is to help us understand how a particular situation may play out, to find guidance, and tell us what the future could bring. However, this particular form of lithomancy which I will discuss here is not primarily focused on divining the future. Rather, it can help you understand the present and what you should be doing (or not doing) to improve your health and wellbeing. We can then use it to heal, to inspire, and to help us maintain balance within ourselves. Self-care has never been more important and the world can be a stressful place sometimes. More emphasis is being put on the importance of mental and emotional health, which I whole-heartedly agree with. Balancing the energies within our body can have a great impact on our overall well-being, which in turn can have a positive influence over our physical health. Our spiritual health is an important part of our overall health and should not be overlooked.

This set consists of twelve stones (including a personal stone), and you create them, cast them, and interpret them in the same way you would for any other lithomancy kit. It is a great little practice that can be used every day if you wish.

I find two types of question work best with this:

*Where should I direct my energy today?*
*Where is my energy being blocked?*

Whilst these sound like the same question, there is a subtle difference. 'Where should I direct my energy' is not asking 'what do I need to fix'. We are asking what should be my biggest focus. This first question is great for short-term goals or if you are generally in a good place and are just looking for some additional guidance. However, if you have found yourself out of sorts for a while or if there are circumstances which seem to be bringing you down regularly, then focusing on clearing blockages (question two) to create a strong, healthy foundation, would be the best approach.

The above questions are the two I use regularly but you can ask anything you want so long as it is in keeping with the theme of this set.

As well as a personal stone, there are seven stones which represent the chakras and four stones which represent the energy of the elements. I will go through the keywords and messages of each stone and then take you through some examples from readings I have done so you can see how it can be used in practice.

## Chakra Stone Meanings

### Root Chakra Stone
Keywords
  Stability
  Security
  Survival
  Ancestral memories
  Basic needs to be fulfilled
  Independence
  Self sufficiency
  Physical strength

Fortitude
Control
Finding direction
Think for ourselves
Selfishness
Co-dependency due to feeling a lack of connection with
ourselves

This stone deals with survival and making sure that we have
the resources necessary to be able to make it through in this
world. It signifies that we need to make sure our basic needs
are being met; shelter, food, heat, etc. In the 21st century, these
needs might not be as easy as you would think to achieve. They
can also be a lot more complex. 'Shelter' doesn't simply mean a
roof over your head but the physical condition of your house,
the relationships you have with the people you share it with, the
financial responsibilities that come with it, etc. Similarly, 'food'
doesn't just mean 'you have food' – is that food nutritious, is it
affordable, easy to obtain, etc.? This stone signifies that it may
be time to go back to basics and make sure these fundamental
needs are being met.

This energy of the root chakra also represents physical
strength, fortitude, and can put us in touch with our most basic
instincts and motivations.

It focuses on the need to develop stability before you progress.
Do you have a solid foundation from which to build up from? If
not, then spend some time laying the groundwork for whatever
it is you wish to succeed in. When this stone appears in a reading,
take a look at the stones around it as it may give you an idea as
to what will help you achieve this security.

All of this can come together to help us become independent
and self-sufficient. At the end of the day support from those
around you is great, but you need to be confident you have the
wherewithal to go at it alone if needs be. Through ensuring that

our basic needs are met and we have these strong foundations to build up, we can find our own direction and think for ourselves.

Of course, too much, or not enough root chakra energy can lead to some less than desired traits, and this stone may appear as a warning. If this chakra is blocked then you may find that you start to experience co-dependency on others, born from the fact that you feel a lack of connection with yourself. If this chakra is overactive then you may find it manifests in selfishness.

**Sacral Chakra Stone**
Keywords
    Physical sensation
    Sexual desire
    How we fit in in the world
    How we present ourselves to others
    How we interact with others on a more 'superficial' level –
    how we impress on others
    Manage our 'immediate' emotions in a healthy way
    Fantasy
    Creativity
    Pursuing hobbies and interests
    Co-dependency due to feeling a lack of connection with others
    Emotionally out of control, or on the other end of the scale,
    completely apathetic to everyone
    Over indulging in fantasy, imagination, or a complete lack
    of it

When this stone appears in a reading, it may be because you have been questioning where you fit into the world. The world is a large place, and sometimes it can make us feel very small. It can be easy to feel overwhelmed and wonder how we fit in in the grand scheme of things – what is our purpose on this earth?

It can also cause us to question how we present ourselves to others. Do you find yourself trying to fill a particular role in your friendship group or at work for example? Do you sometimes feel that you are putting on an act and that the person you present yourself as is disingenuous to whom you really are? Of course sometimes we are in a position where we need to impress people, such as during a job interview, and so need an awareness of how to conduct ourselves that may not be entirely true to our nature. Take some time to consider how you present yourself and how you interact with others to achieve your goals – that goal doesn't have to be to get a promotion or a pay rise, it could simply be to make some new friends! Humans are largely social creatures and often we want others to think well of us and enjoy our company. Are you comfortable with this version of yourself, and will it help you achieve your end goals?

Physical sensation and relationships, as well as sexual desire are also governed by this energy. It can help us ensure we don't overindulge in physical pleasures and help us appreciate the physicality of the world around us. Through the sacral chakra we can learn to manage our 'immediate', or surface emotions in a healthy way (as opposed to the heart chakra which deals with deeper emotions).

This energy also encourages the fantastic and exploring our imaginations. It can bring a lively enthusiasm which helps us pursue our hobbies and interests, and find passion for our personal projects again.

Negative manifestations can of course occur. Where this energy is blocked or lacking, it can lead to co-dependency in your relationships. This co-dependency is caused by a lack of connection with others, and so when we do eventually form this connection with another person we can become overly reliant on them for our own self-fulfilment.

Alternatively you could feel completely apathetic and switched off. If there is an abundance of this energy in your life then you could find that you spend a lot of time with your head in the clouds, ignoring reality. Or you could find that you are emotionally out of control and have trouble expressing these emotions to yourself and others. When this stone appears, use your intuition to determine if it is in fact a warning about any of these more negative behaviors.

**The Solar Plexus Chakra Stone**
Keywords
Will
Personal power
Responsibility for actions and their consequences
Clarity in decision making
Comfortable with our own thoughts and opinions
Self-assurance
Confidence
Independence
Self-discipline
Helping us determine our identity
Mental faculties
Putting plans into reality
Unhealthy attitude towards authority and control
Being unable to take responsibility for actions/consequences
Helplessness
Obsessing about minor details
Feeling directionless
Never following through with plans

The energy of the solar plexus stone is focused around our personal identity. Where the sacral chakra energy helped us realize ourselves in the external world, this energy helps us realize ourselves in our own internal world. It emphasizes will and personal power and brings confidence and self-assurance. As we journey through this discovery of the self we find our confidence increases and we become more comfortable in our own thoughts and opinions. This confidence in our own self can bring clarity in decision making and encourage us to take responsibility for our actions and their consequences. As such, when this stone appears, issues of personal identity may be at the fore.

This energy is also associated with our mental faculties. Anything that involves memory, information retention, problem solving, academia and such, can be improved upon if we have a balance of this energy in our lives.

A combination of this comfort with our own identity, confidence in our own actions and decisions, and increased mental capacity can help us make some well-formed plans and then bring those plans into reality. It brings us the practical mind-set we need to start manifesting our desires out into the real world.

You may find that if you have a blockage or lack of energy in this area that you are unable to take responsibility for your actions and their consequences. You may feel directionless, like you are unable to follow through with any of your plans. If you have an overabundance of this energy then you may find yourself developing an unhealthy attitude towards authority and control or that you begin to obsess over the tiniest of details.

**Heart Chakra Stone**
Keywords
    Compassion
    Forgiveness
    Overcoming grief
    Emotional healing
    Selflessness
    Beauty
    Transformation
    Change
    Making peace
    Victim/savior complex

Co-dependency, caring too much what others think of us
Isolation
Holding grudges

The energy of the heart chakra stone is very much focused on our emotions and creating balance within our emotional selves. Where the sacral chakra focuses on 'surface' emotions, the heart chakra deals with that which dwells deep in our subconscious. If this stone appears in your reading then take a look at the emotions you harbour. Are there any that don't serve you or are a cause for negativity? Feelings such as anger, envy, or jealousy are perfectly natural, but if we dwell on them rather than dealing with them then they can cause us real harm in the long term.

The heart chakra helps us to take any negative feelings we may be harboring and to replace them with compassion and forgiveness. Through this, it can help us to become more selfless and transcend the ego and allow us to see the beauty in all things. Focus on the good that you have in your life and practice gratitude rather than focusing on what you don't have.

This energy can also appear if we are going through a period of change. Change can be upsetting, especially sudden or unexpected change. This stone helps remind us that sometimes it is better not to fight change, but to go with the flow and make sure we are managing our emotional responses to that change in a healthy manner.

If you are experiencing blockages in the heart chakra, it can lead to holding on to any negative feelings and developing grudges. You could become withdrawn and isolated. There is also the possibility that you could develop a 'victim complex'. On the opposite end of the spectrum, an overabundance of this energy can lead to a savior complex, or you could find yourself becoming too over-emotional and taking on others problems.

**Throat Chakra Stone**

Keywords

    Communication

    Expression

    Telling the truth

    Finding the right words/communicating in the right way

    Courage to speak up

    Communicating with the spirit world

    Creativity

    Bringing creativity into the real world

    Lying

    Not saying anything of value

    Gossiping

The energy of the throat chakra stone governs our communication and creativity. Communication is an important aspect of our lives. From the words we say (or don't say), to the way in which we intone them, communication can often make or break relationships, work deals, and other aspects of our lives. It is important to know when to talk and when to listen. It is also important to make sure we get our points across succinctly, using appropriate language depending on our audience, and speak with clarity and truth.

Sometimes communication can be difficult or scary, especially public speaking or when talking to people you may not know very well. Strengthening this chakra can help our words flow freely and bring us confidence in how we communicate. It is also the seat of our creative expression and can manifest itself through more than just spoken word; it could be through writing, through music, or some other artistic medium.

The throat chakra governs not just communication in the physical world but also communication with our guides and the spirit world. Is there a message that you are refusing to hear?

A blockage in this area can cause fear and anxiety around

communication. You may find yourself telling lies or untruths to avoid having to own up or take responsibility for your thoughts and actions. An overabundance of energy in this area can cause an inclination towards gossip or the ability to talk and talk without saying anything of value.

**Third Eye Chakra Stone**
Keywords
    Seeing the unseen
    Spirituality, our Higher Selves
    Helping us recognize energy shifts
    Wisdom
    Intellect
    Growth through learning and life experiences
    Trusting our intuition
    Feeling stuck in the daily grind
    Dependency on the material

The third eye chakra energy stone represents our spirituality as a whole. Connecting with your higher selves is necessary to proceed and succeed. Trusting your intuition is key.

The energy of this chakra can help us see the unseen. Often this phrase is used in a metaphysical sense, in the context of seeing and communicating with spirits and such. In this instance that is indeed one meaning, but it also refers to being unable to see the bigger picture. Expand your vision, try to view the situation from all sides, and see if there is anything that you may be missing before you decide the best course of action.

Wisdom and intellect are also governed by the third eye chakra. By connecting with our higher selves and listening to our intuition, we put ourselves on the path to acquire these attributes. It teaches us to learn and grow from our experiences if we wish to progress and find balance and peace in our lives. As such, when it appears in a reading, reflect and see if there are any lessons that you may be resisting.

With an emphasis on all things spiritual, strengthening this chakra can also help us recognize subtle shifts in our energy and the environment around us. Take care to ensure that you aren't exposing yourself to toxicity and negativity which can wear you down.

When this energy is blocked we can feel stuck in the daily grind of life or find ourselves becoming too reliant on material possessions. On the other end of the scale, when we have an overabundance of energy, we can feel unattached and ungrounded from reality.

**Crown Chakra Stone**
Keywords
   Releasing negative patterns
   Finding a higher purpose
   Connection with the world
   Freedom
   Inner peace
   Balance
   Transcendence

The crown chakra energy stone symbolizes that there is some sort of 'higher purpose' that you are striving for. This isn't necessarily some grand or noble endeavor, but rather a goal or dream you have which you wish to pursue. If you don't have one, then this can be a sign that it is time to set yourself some goals and aim high.

Inner peace and balance is governed by this energy, and the releasing of negative patterns which may hold us back from. It can also represent the need to deal with any bad habits or such that may be holding you back from progressing with your 'higher purpose'. This higher purpose and the attainment of such, as well as this emphasis on finding peace and balance, can help free us from the constraints of the mundane world. It gives us something to aim for and can help us transcend the norm. When this energy is blocked we can feel like we are floating aimlessly through life or struggle to find the motivation or energy to achieve anything. Where there is an overabundance of this energy we may find that we are too invested in our goals, to the detriment of everything else in our lives. We may be prone to arrogance, believing that our way is the only way, and the only true, noble purpose in life.

**Earth Stone**
Keywords
    Serious look at life; foundations, priorities
    New ideas, seeds of growth
    Look for that which is sustainable
    Take some time out to recuperate

Where the earth stone appears in a reading, it emphasizes the need to make sure that you have built up strong foundations in whatever you are pursuing. For example, if it appears next to the throat chakra stone then it could mean the need to ensure that you have done the necessary planning and 'foundation building' before embarking on a creative endeavor or communicating any ideas you have. It is associated with new ideas and planting the seeds of growth.

It also teaches us to think long term and aim for that which is sustainable. Short term pleasures are gratuitous; if you really want to make a long-lasting change then you need to make sure your approach is also long-term. For example, if you have decided you want to commit to writing a book and decide to write 2,000 words a day for the next six months, do you really think you will have the time or energy to stick to that?

The earth stone energy can also tell us that there is a need to take some time out, rest and recuperate. Mental, physical, and emotional burnout is one of those things that can build up slowly over time, or it can hit us suddenly. Where it appears, you may be close to that burnout whether you realize it or not, so make sure you give yourself time to rest and recover.

**Air Stone**
Keywords
Blow away those cobwebs!
Embracing creativity, especially the arts
Sociability
Trying something new

The energy of the air stone is an uplifting one. It revitalizes our mental faculties and helps rejuvenate us when we find ourselves in a bit of a slump. The air stone tells us it is time to pull ourselves out of the lethargy we may be feeling and put our focus towards something productive! This is especially true of mental pursuits and anything that encourages creativity. It can be difficult to motivate ourselves at times but the energy of the air stone promises us that is what is needed at the moment. It may be that it is time to throw yourself into something new. If you are already in the middle of some sort of creative endeavour, or one which requires a lot of mental effort, it may be that you need to find a new approach to help you progress. Try to recapture the passion you felt for the project when you first started it and blow away those cobwebs!

The uplifting energy of this element also aids us in social situations, and teaches us to enjoy others' company and find support from our social networks. If you are struggling to motivate yourself, seek out like-minded people and let them inspire you.

**Fire Stone**
Keywords

Perseverance
Action
Putting yourself out there
Confidence in all things
Passion

The energy of the fire stone teaches us perseverance. Life is not always easy, and even the most enjoyable of activities can become a bit of a slog at times. This energy encourages us to keep going, to keep at it, because it will pay off eventually. It brings us strength and teaches us to be confident in our abilities.

When the fire stone appears, it is time for action. Planning and strategizing is all well and good but you will achieve very little unless you put the work in. If you are waiting for the right time then there is no time like the present. Even if it means starting small, this is the time to start actually working towards your goals. Putting yourself out there can be scary but embrace the passionate energy this element provides and draw on its confidence to make your move.

**Water Stone**
Keywords
Emotions
Nurturing
Withdrawing from the world
Self-love

Like the tides of the seas rise and fall, so too can our own energy. When this stone appears, it is time to find balance, especially when it comes to your emotions. It may be that you need to withdraw from the world for a bit and reflect on what it is you are trying to achieve and how you are trying to achieve it. Don't be afraid to take this time out and look inward at how your current situation may be affecting you.

When this stone appears it is a sign that you need to start looking after yourself. Self-love and making sure you are taking the appropriate steps to care for yourself and look out for your own needs is very important. Where this stone talks of nurturing, it is most often nurturing ourselves that it refers to. Take that time to re-evaluate your current situation and ensure that you are protecting yourself before you progress.

## Example Readings

When it comes to interpreting these readings, you do so in exactly the same way as you would a traditional divination reading. However, there are a couple of key differences I have noted.

The first is that depending on the question you ask and how balanced your energies already are, you could find that your reading gives you essentially a 'one word' answer. You may find that just one or two stones fall close enough to the personal stone to feel relevant. Or, even if more stones do feel closer, there will generally be one or two stones which feel of primary importance. There is nothing wrong with this – I experience it often when asking where I should be directing my energies day-to-day. Or you may find that it does indeed provide you with a very in depth reading as is common when using lithomancy for divination purposes.

If you are using this set every day, you may get very similar messages crop up over a period of time. For example, when I was working on the final manuscript for this book, most days I would find the crown chakra stone and the throat chakra stone falling near each other. Often, they would form a triangle shape with either the sacral chakra stone, the root chakra stone, or the air element stone. This was always very promising and symbolized that I needed to tap into my higher self to fulfil this 'higher purpose' (remember, this higher purpose can be any goal you have set your mind to) to help fuel my creative expression.

When the throat and crown stones fell with the root stone, it symbolized the need to make sure I had laid the necessary groundwork and done the proper planning. As such, I made sure to read all the guidance that had been sent to me before I started the formal process of submitting this book. It was a good job I did, as there were definitely tasks I had overlooked that would have meant I missed the deadlines I had set myself had I ignored them! With the sacral chakra stone they represented the need to reconnect with my higher self to find the enthusiasm and passion for this 'hobby' again, to fuel my creative expression. Finally, with the air element stone, they similarly represented the need to 'blow away the cobwebs' and carry on with the book.

In another reading I performed around this time the air stone fell upside down next to the sacral chakra stone, and then the water stone fell next to the sacral chakra stone. Together they formed an arch curving slightly upwards. It was actually the sacral chakra stone which fell opposite my personal stone, and so this felt like the most important part of this arc.

My intuition told me that the air stone upside down represented that I was trying to find the energy to get creative and try something new, but I was struggling. With the sacral chakra stone being next, I got the impression that this was related to hobbies and other interests, what with the air stone representing creativity and trying something new. So clearly I was struggling to find the motivation to indulge in any of my hobbies. The water stone then told me that the way to resolve this was to take some time out, withdraw, and practice some self-care first to help regain this passion.

The second difference I have noticed using lithomancy to help with energy healing is a particular layout which occurs often. It is not one I see very often in divination readings and feels very specific to this way of using lithomancy for energy healing.

If you are using the stones to work out where energy is blocked as opposed to where you should be directing your energies, oftentimes I will find a multitude of stones centred around one particular stone (or stones). In one reading for example, the air stone fell close to my personal stone, and then above this fell several of the chakra stones in a straight line. I could feel that each of these chakra stones were related to the air stone beneath them, as opposed to each other. Bringing the energy of air into my life would therefore help to unblock the different chakra energies represented by the stones in this line. Similarly, I have had two or three stones fall in a line above the personal stone, and then the other stones falling in an evenly spread out format above them. It felt very clear that again the reading was telling me to focus on bringing the energies of those particular two or three stones into my life to help unblock and energize the other chakras.

This is a great method of lithomancy to practice alongside a more traditional divination method and one which is quite easy to interpret. The messages it delivers can be invaluable, and can really help you manage your energy and well-being day-today.

# Chapter 6

# Final Word

Lithomancy is a lot of fun; from creating your own sets, to the actual readings themselves, it is a great divination method to pick up and have a go with. Best of all, it really can be tailored to you and your preferences and symbolism and can grow with you as you become more skilled in your practice. There is so much flexibility in it that it can really allow you to be creative and explore what works and what doesn't work for you. Hopefully having read this book you will feel confident in choosing your own stones, cleansing them, assigning meanings to them, and performing readings for yourself and others.

Interpreting your readings is the key and it can seem daunting at first. If you don't pick it up right away, don't worry. Lithomancy really is something which can be learned, and your intuition will grow the more you practice. Feel free to start small. Using the yes/no stones, using a segmented chart, or even just working off of keywords for your first few readings are all a great way to build up your confidence and get to know your stones.

Finally, trust your intuition. I know I've spoken a lot in this book about how listening to your intuition is key but it cannot be overstated. If you find you are struggling then spend some time meditating with your stones. Do you need to tweak the messages? Are you perhaps missing some messages from your set and need to add to it, or maybe there are stones in there which aren't really serving any purpose? Don't be afraid to play around and add new stones or take them away from your set.

I hope you've found this book useful, and I wish you all the best on your own journey into lithomancy!

# Appendix: Keywords and Associations

**Love, Relationships, Self-Love, Friendships:** Symbols that are associated with all types of love, friendship, and relationships include hearts, roses, birds such as the swan or the dove, and the Claddagh (two hands holding a heart with a crown). Crystals that are a pink or red colour such as rose quartz, garnet, or emerald are also suitable for love and relationships; additionally, moonstone is good for self-love and citrine, ametrine, or carnelian good for friendships. The cockle shell is also associated with love.

**Health:** Green or blue coloured stones, a stone with symbols of health drawn on (such as the Caduceus) or an equal armed cross, green or blue crystals such as aventurine, snakes, a periwinkle shell.

**Wealth:** Green coloured stones, a stone with symbols of currency such as the pound/dollar/euro symbols drawn on, a small coin, a small cowry shell, the salmon.

**Career:** Many of the colours and symbols associated with money can also represent career. Colours which represent success, such as gold or orange, can also be used. Suitable gold or orange crystals to consider include sunstone, goldstone, and citrine. Other symbols could include something specific to your career, such as a stethoscope if you are a doctor.

**Travel:** Sea glass, a round stone decorated to look like the earth, or a stone with a mode of transport on such as a plane or boat, a foreign coin, or maybe even a stone that you picked up from a different place you have travelled to.

**Communication:** Blue crystals such as blue lace agate or turquoise are often used to represent communication. Alphabetic characters drawn onto your stone reminiscent of a letter can also help, or the image of a quill.

**Creativity:** Blue crystals such as blue lace agate or lapis lazuli are often used to represent creativity. Other symbols you could find charms of, or draw onto your stones include theatre masks, paintbrushes, palettes, or an easel, or a thread spool.

**Warning/Danger:** Red is often the colour associated with danger, and so red coloured stones and crystals such as jasper would work well. Other symbols associated with warnings or danger include the lightning bolt, exclamation mark, a skull and crossbones, and a cross.

**Burn Out** (as in, you are taking too much on and risking burn-out): Black coloured stones and crystals such as black tourmaline, onyx, or obsidian could work well to represent burn out. There aren't many other traditional symbols that represent burn out, but a used match or burnt down candle could work well as a pictorial representation.

**Happiness:** Yellow or orange coloured stones or crystals such as citrine or carnelian are often used to represent joy and happiness. Other symbols to consider include the sun, flowers, and a smiley face. Symbols often ascribed to peace could also be relevant, such as a yin-yang or the circle split into three equal sections.

**Spirituality/Intuition:** Purple crystals such as amethyst are often used to represent spirituality and intuition, as are clear or white crystals such as selenite or clear quartz. Other symbols you could use include the pentacle, God or Goddess symbols, the moon, a lotus flower, the symbol for Awen or the Triquetra.

**Home Life/Place/Environment:** There are many symbols you

could use depending on your view of 'place'. It could be a house, a temple, or a symbol of traditional domesticity such as a thimble or thread spool. Maybe you associate the home with family, in which case even stick-figures depicting a family drawn onto a stone could suffice.

# MOON
# BOOKS

## PAGANISM & SHAMANISM

What is Paganism? A religion, a spirituality, an alternative belief system, nature worship? You can find support for all these definitions (and many more) in dictionaries, encyclopaedias, and text books of religion, but subscribe to any one and the truth will evade you. Above all Paganism is a creative pursuit, an encounter with reality, an exploration of meaning and an expression of the soul. Druids, Heathens, Wiccans and others, all contribute their insights and literary riches to the Pagan tradition. Moon Books invites you to begin or to deepen your own encounter, right here, right now.

If you have enjoyed this book, why not tell other readers by posting a review on your preferred book site.

**Medicine for the Soul**
The Complete Book of Shamanic Healing
Ross Heaven
All you will ever need to know about shamanic healing and how to
become your own shaman...
Paperback: 978-1-78099-419-2 ebook: 978-1-78099-420-8


**Shaman Pathways – The Druid Shaman**
Exploring the Celtic Otherworld
Danu Forest
A practical guide to Celtic shamanism with exercises and
techniques as well as traditional lore for exploring the Celtic
Otherworld.
Paperback: 978-1-78099-615-8 ebook: 978-1-78099-616-5


**Traditional Witchcraft for the Woods and Forests**
A Witch's Guide to the Woodland with Guided Meditations and
Pathworking
Mélusine Draco
A Witch's guide to walking alone in the woods, with guided
meditations and pathworking.
Paperback: 978-1-84694-803-9 ebook: 978-1-84694-804-6


**Wild Earth, Wild Soul**
A Manual for an Ecstatic Culture
Bill Pfeiffer
Imagine a nature-based culture so alive and so connected,
spreading like wildfire. This book is the first flame...
Paperback: 978-1-78099-187-0 ebook: 978-1-78099-188-7

**Naming the Goddess**
Trevor Greenfield
*Naming the Goddess* is written by over eighty adherents and scholars of Goddess and Goddess Spirituality.
Paperback: 978-1-78279-476-9 ebook: 978-1-78279-475-2


**Shapeshifting into Higher Consciousness**
Heal and Transform Yourself and Our World with Ancient Shamanic and Modern Methods
Llyn Roberts
Ancient and modern methods that you can use every day to transform yourself and make a positive difference in the world.
Paperback: 978-1-84694-843-5 ebook: 978-1-84694-844-2


Readers of ebooks can buy or view any of these bestsellers by clicking on the live link in the title. Most titles are published in paperback and as an ebook. Paperbacks are available in traditional bookshops. Both print and ebook formats are available online.

Find more titles and sign up to our readers' newsletter at
http://www.johnhuntpublishing.com/paganism
Follow us on Facebook at https://www.facebook.com/MoonBooks
and Twitter at https://twitter.com/MoonBooksJHP